D0913167

Benedetto Croce Reconsidered

Benedetto Croce Reconsidered

Truth and Error in
Theories of Art,
Literature, and History

M. E. MOSS
WITH A FOREWORD BY MAURICE MANDELBAUM

UNIVERSITY PRESS OF NEW ENGLAND
HANOVER AND LONDON, 1987

Randall Library UNC-W

UNIVERSITY PRESS OF NEW ENGLAND
Brandeis University
Brown University
Clark University
University of Connecticut
Dartmouth College
University of New Hampshire
University of Rhode Island
Tufts University
University of Vermont

© 1987 by University Press of New England

All rights reserved. Except for brief quotation in critical articles or reviews, this book, or parts thereof, must not be reproduced in any form without permission in writing from the publisher. For further information contact University Press of New England, Hanover, NH 03755.

Printed in the United States of America

LIBRARY OF CONGRESS CATALOGING-IN-PUBLICATION DATA

Moss, M. E.
    Benedetto Croce reconsidered.

    Bibliography: p.
    Includes index.
    1. Croce, Benedetto, 1866–1952   I. Title
B3614.C74M63   1987   195   86–22399
ISBN 0–87451–399–5

5   4   3   2   1

Photograph of Croce courtesy of Dr. Ernesto Paolozzi

B
3614
.C74
M63
1987

Contents

Foreword

Considering the unique place that Benedetto Croce occupied in the intellectual and cultural life of Italy for some fifty years, it may seem surprising that apart from a few striking fragments excavated from his writings on aesthetics and on the theory of historiography almost no American philosophers, and only a few intellectual historians, have been concerned with his work.

One contributing factor had been a linguistic barrier. Although the four books that form the cornerstones of his system have been translated into English (not always happily), his many lesser writings that serve to illustrate and illuminate their significance have, in general, not been translated, and their sheer volume has discouraged careful exploitation. Consequently, almost the sole interpretive studies that have appeared since his death are in Italian, and insofar as they presuppose a good deal of prior knowledge of and sympathy for his position, they have not been effective in making his thought more accessible to others. In addition, although we are presently witnessing a widespread revival of interest in Hegel among philosophers who formerly neglected the German philosopher, Croce's revisions of Hegelianism tended to strip it of its emphasis on the ways in which the dialectic manifests itself concretely in experience, thus robbing it of much that contributes to its present appeal.

The most serious impediment to an understanding of Croce lies, however, in the way in which some of his doctrines, taken out of the context of his system, have been seized upon and made to serve purposes for which they were not entirely well suited. His use of the concept of intuition, for example, is most often treated as if it were solely—or even primarily—a concept to be used in a theory of art, rather than as the basis of his entire epistemological position. Similarly, his doctrine that history is the re-creation of past experience in the mind of the historian, and that all genuine history (as distinct from mere chronicle) is therefore contemporary history, has sometimes been treated as posing special problems for the theory of historiography. These problems, however, follow from the basic nature of Croce's idealism and are equally characteristic of other fields of inquiry and discourse.

It is only when one traces the development of Croce's views, placing them within the total context of his thought, and clarifies the terminology that he used in expressing them, that one can arrive at an estimate of his contributions and his failures as a philosopher. On the basis of her examination of the whole range of Croce's work, and her knowledge of the ablest recent Italian Crocean scholarship, Myra Moss has been able to offer the reader a balanced portrayal of Croce's entire system. In my opinion, there is no other book in English that in this respect serves the Anglo-American reader as well.

MAURICE MANDELBAUM

Preface

The aim of this work is not primarily biographical or historical. I highlight only those events in the life of the Italian philosopher Benedetto Croce (1866–1952) that have provided major stimuli to his thought. My goal instead is a critical one. It is to distinguish what still "lives," to use Croce's term, in his philosophy from what may be advantageously discarded, that is, the idealistic implications that *he* drew from his tenet that historical knowledge is self-knowledge. I argue that Croce's idealist epistemological assumptions, along with the coherence theory of truth that he derived from them, are not viable. Nevertheless his categorial conception of error provides a genuine contribution to contemporary philosophical thought. And finally, Croce's view that philosophy amounted to methodology and that the philosopher's task was to delineate "categories of the real" is indeed consistent with the historical nature of reality.

Chapter 1 presents a biography with highlights of Croce's career. The chapter that follows gives an outline of the Crocean philosophy. I wish to provide the reader with a general understanding of Croce's view to serve as a frame of reference for the specific problems that I have chosen to treat. Here I adopt Croce's own method of inquiry and begin with a discussion of the fundamental expressions of consciousness and their relations to one another. Human theoretical (cognitive) and practical (volitional) activities are treated in the order of their dependency, according to Croce's methodology. First of all, I consider the theoretic activity of intuition. Croce described it as "autonomous," and as not explicitly involving other kinds of conscious expression. Second, I discuss the "pure concepts," inasmuch as these were the logical expressions that originated from intuitions. Finally, I treat the sphere of the practical in its economic and ethical forms, since their occurrence presupposed theoretic activity. According to Croce, on the one hand, will depended upon thought, and on the other, volition was a necessary prerequisite to knowledge. Croce's mature doctrine stressed the interrelatedness of the expressions of human spirit, such that ethical will provided the "material" to be transformed by intuition into cognition. However, each of these activities of consciousness—intuitional, logical, economic, and ethical—remained distinguishable; only intuition could be considered in separation from the rest. In subsequent chapters my detailed explanation of Croce's elements of judgment, intuition (subject) and concept (predicate), likewise follows the Crocean order of their phenomenological dependency. I next treat types of judgment, then examine the coherence theory of truth and the categorial conception of error applicable to them. Evaluation of Croce's starting point and method are reserved until the final chapter, which estimates his contributions to contemporary methodology.

During the course of my exposition of Croce's philosophy, I treat some inconsistencies and problems of interpretation that arise within its framework. Illustrations of his theory are drawn from his aesthetics, literary criticism, and conception of history. A good case indeed could be made that his philosophical concepts evolved from his extensive activity as a literary critic and historian. Ultimately, changes in theory probably were forced from praxis. This interpretation is one with which Croce himself would have concurred, since according to his philosophy, the rhythm of life consisted of a dialectical movement of the human spirit between theory and praxis, praxis and theory. Such a theme, however, would form the topic for another book and is not developed here. The dialectical relationship between theory and praxis characteristic of Croce's work at times lent itself to ambiguity and inconsistency. In subsequent chapters, which discuss the elements of judgment, I note these inconsistencies. Occasionally, they can be resolved without doing violence to Croce's fundamental position. Other difficulties of exposition include ambiguous language. Although I attempt to clarify Croce's terminology, I hope that I do not render his concepts and philosophic alterations more clear than in fact they were. Problems also arise from condensation of extensive material. The volumes of Croce published by Laterza numbered twenty-seven in 1922, forty-eight in 1940, and fifty-five in 1950. These figures exclude pamphlets and brief monographs. Some scholars are so little acquainted with Croce's works that they write as if he were a nineteenth-century scholar whose major work lay in history, or in aesthetics, or in literary criticism, whereas it occurred mainly during the twentieth century and included these disciplines as well as much more. It is thus easy to become lost in a forest of detail when treating a prolific writer such as Croce. I think it helpful to single out major conceptions such as truth and error and to follow their adventures in his aesthetics and theory of history. It was in these disciplines that Croce best illustrated his philosophy. Indeed Croce himself urged that philosophic inquiry be stimulated by particular problems and questions.

Since the 1960s, when this book began to take shape, I have been aided by many institutions and kind individuals. In America, Professor Maurice Mandelbaum first suggested the subject at The Johns Hopkins University. He has encouraged and helped me during these many years. Professors Victor Lowe, Albert Hammond, Kingsley Price, and George Boas were also influential in forming my thought. Persons who were kind enough to read and comment on the manuscript included Professors G. N. G. Orsini, A. R. Caponigri, Frederick Sontag, John Roth, Richard and Louise Lillard, Don Abbott, and Giuseppe Mazzotta. Special thanks are due to Professor Andrew Rolle, who has offered constructive criticism of all the major drafts. Professor George K. Plochmann and Mrs. Corinna Marsh helped considerably in editing content, structure, and style.

In Rome, Professor Guido Calogero, his wife, Maria Comandini, and Miss Nina Ruffini were my first Italian guides through the labyrinth of Croce's work. Subsequently my understanding deepened through conversation with Professors Gennaro Sasso and Antonio Capizzi, and more recently by means of correspondence with Dr. Ernesto Paolozzi. None of these persons is responsible for whatever shortcomings exist in this book.

The libraries at the University of Rome in Italy, The Johns Hopkins University, Stanford University, the University of California at Los Angeles, the Claremont Colleges, Occidental College, and the Huntington Library made available many of the sources on which this work rests. Claremont McKenna College contributed some of the funding necessary for its publication. Pat Padilla, Carol Bovett, Lillis Walls, and Janet Gray assisted with the typing of the drafts. And finally, I should like to thank the staff members of this publisher for their efficiency, courtesy, and careful editing of the manuscript during the final stages of its preparation.

Benedetto Croce Reconsidered

1

Croce's Life

Benedetto Croce was one of the most creative and polemical thinkers of his time. With unique insight and rare courage he contested intellectual trends then accepted by Italian philosophers. These trends included orthodox Hegelian idealism, Marxism, and neopositivism. Croce's theory was that the past, in order to make itself understood, had to be integrated with the present. The generations were bound together by history, which gave concrete meaning to individual worth.

Croce's guiding principle became a moral element in human activity, which was expressed by the concept of liberty. In his own work, indeed, he exhibited an *impegno* or commitment whose intensity never lessened. A searching look into the major determinants of Croce's distinguished career illuminates the intellectual development of this important Italian philosopher, hitherto so little understood outside his native country.

Early Influences: The Ischia Earthquake

Croce's early life remained at the epicenter of all his subsequent thought. In 1883, when he was seventeen years old, a tragedy left deep scars upon the sensitive and thoughtful youth. Unfortunately, otherwise excellent biographies, such as Cecil Sprigge's *Benedetto Croce: Man and Thinker,*[1] do not treat the influence that this tragedy exercised upon

Croce's life. Although other works, including Fausto Nicolini's *Benedetto Croce* and Italo De Feo's *Benedetto Croce e il suo mondo,* acknowledge its deep effects, they fail to link them to his philosophical development. Since ancient times the town of Casamicciola, situated on the island of Ischia near Naples, has been jolted by severe earthquakes. By 1881 this geographical area already had been two-thirds destroyed during such violent upheavals. Two years later, however, tourists began to return there in order to enjoy its beauty and the health-giving properties of the local waters. Among these visitors were Croce's parents, Pasquale Croce and Luisa Sipari Croce, as well as Benedetto and his younger sister Maria. They stayed in a hotel (Villa Verde) while Croce's brother Alfonso was away at boarding school. Croce recalled that on July 28, 1883, he and his family, having completed their dinner, all retired to the same room.[2] That evening his father was writing a letter; Croce, seated in front of him, read silently. His mother and sister were conversing in a corner of the room. Suddenly they heard a prolonged rumble. At the same moment the building shook under them. Croce saw his father jump to his feet and his sister hurl herself into the arms of his mother. He instinctively ran out onto the adjoining terrace, which then crumbled beneath him. Croce lost consciousness. When he revived he was buried up to his neck. Dazed, he could not determine where he had fallen and felt as if he might be dreaming.

Croce called for help, for both himself and his father—whose voice he heard at lengthening intervals, growing always weaker. In spite of every effort, he could not free himself from the ruins. The quake was followed by a torrential rain, which almost drowned the young boy, who remained trapped under the fallen rubble for more than twelve hours. Finally, sometime during the next evening, Croce was rescued by two soldiers. Much later the dead bodies of his father and his mother, still embracing Croce's only sister, were removed from the debris. Croce was transported to Naples by his cousin Paolo Petroni and underwent two operations for a fractured leg and arm. He subsequently wrote that his injuries had provided some solace for his guilt as the lone survivor of his family. However, the results of the surgery were not entirely successful; afterwards he would walk with a slight limp.

Croce had just earned great praise for Latin and Greek examinations when he suffered the Ischia earthquake in 1883. His longtime friend and biographer, Fausto Nicolini, revealed that even during Croce's last years he refrained from speaking of his family's suffocation, so intense was the trauma in its retelling and reexperiencing.[3] In a British Broadcasting Company commemoration on December 25, 1952, Professor Guido Calogero recalled Croce as a "sad man—his early adult life stood under the shadow of the sudden extinction of his whole family in the earthquake of Casamicciola, and even the fragment of his diaries which has been published reveals a melancholic mind."[4]

Parental Influences

Clinical studies have shown that the more favorable are the childhood influences—especially parental models and immediate relations—the more likely the survivor will adapt to trauma.[5] What were such factors in Croce's early life? Croce's father, Pasquale, was a descendant of an Abruzzi family, which had migrated to Naples during the preceding generation. His mother, Luisa Sipari, was from the remote mountain village of Pescasseroli in the Abruzzi region of southern Italy. During a cholera epidemic in Naples, both parents moved to Pescasseroli, where Croce was born on February 25, 1866. He was their third child, having been preceded by a boy, whose name also had been Benedetto, and a girl, both of whom had died as babies. Benedetto's parents later had four other children: two died as infants; the other two were Alfonso, born in 1867, and Maria, born in 1870.

During the long winter months of Pescasseroli, the surrounding snow-covered mountains prohibited access to the town from the outside world. The internal character and intimacy of Croce's family were important elements in his nurturing. The organization of the household reflected tranquillity, order, and persistent hard work. Croce himself was to express those qualities in his prolific literary and historical writings. His earliest memories were of his father industriously enclosed in a study amid administrative papers.[6] He devoted himself to the affairs of the family estates, a task that much later Croce's brother Alfonso would assume. From his mother, Croce gained a love of art and literature and an appreciation of classical monuments. She frequently took her son to see the ancient buildings and historical records of the Neapolitan churches. Croce was also a voracious reader of historical romances, especially those by Sir Walter Scott. Industry, integrity, and a high regard for history's effect upon the present were the parental qualities that Croce, scholar, critic, and historian, would bring to his work.

Croce's Crisis of Faith

At the age of nine Croce entered a Catholic school in Naples, the Collegio della Carità, frequented by the children of Bourbon aristocrats. Although it was not a Jesuit institution, the boarding school was managed by Catholic priests and it offered a moral and religious education to its young students. Perhaps here lay a source of Croce's philosophic vision that the human spirit was unified and vitalized by the moral side of us all:

> A man would not be moral without the capacities for reason and imagination, for intellectual and artistic experience; he could not philosophise unless he had a strain of poetry and a strong and delicate conscience; each several activity draws its specific energy from the spiritual unity, morality, purely moral, rejecting the inroads of sophistic logic, the other, purely speculative, uncontaminated by misplaced edification. So, too, it is impossible to be a poet or an artist without being in the first place a man nourished by thought and by experience of moral ideals and conflicts.[7]

While Croce was attending secondary school, his passion for literature, first awakened by his mother, flourished. Croce described himself as a good scholar, although somewhat arrogant and undisciplined. His schooling, administered and taught as it was along lines adopted three centuries prior, made these years and those that followed at the *liceo* (high school) relatively happy ones.[8] Nevertheless, during this period

Croce began to question his Catholicism. Until that time he had been educated in a rigorously Catholic family and school, and he himself had been a fervent believer. His religious crisis occurred at the end of 1879 and was prompted by lectures on the philosophy of religion given by the director of his *collegio,* Father Attansio. Croce described his crisis as somewhat painful, for he vacillated between his doubts and his resolution to be devout until, he wrote,

> my thoughts wandered elsewhere, life claimed my attention, I no longer asked myself whether I believed or no, even while through force of habit or for the sake of convenience I kept up certain religious observances; till at last, little by little, I let even these drop, and a day came when I saw, and told myself plainly, that I was done with my religious beliefs.[9]

Apparently Croce's childhood religion was no aid to him in his subsequent working through of loss and reparation.

The Liceo Genovese

Croce completed his subsequent schooling at the Liceo Genovese in Naples. There he neglected his study of mathematics and natural sciences—in part as a result of little interest and also as an expression of his poetic and romantic spirit. By 1882 the young student had read and reread works by Francisco De Sanctis and Giosué Carducci. From the former Croce gained guiding principles for use in literary criticism. However, it would be some time before Croce would develop the implications of De Sanctis's central idea "that art is not a work of reflection and logic, nor yet a product of skill, but pure and spontaneous imaginative form." According to Croce himself, "the philosophical basis of this idea, its necessary implications, the general conception to which it belongs, and its bearings on judgment and action, all these I saw darkly, if at all, and only began by degrees to discern as time went on."[10] By then he was much more attracted by the violent and combative attitudes of Carducci, which apparently he tried to imitate "in a contempt for the frivolous and self-indulgent manners of the fashionable world."[11]

A New Home: Rome and Silvio Spaventa

After the disaster at Casamicciola, Silvio Spaventa, a son of Maria Croce, who was a sister of Croce's paternal grandfather,[12] moved Benedetto and his brother, Alfonso, to his home in Rome. Croce had already attended some lectures on formal logic given at the University of Naples by Silvio's brother, Bertrando Spaventa, who had professed a neo-Hegelian philosophy.[13] Indeed Bertrando has been described as the greatest Italian exponent of Hegel during the nineteenth century. Croce attended his lectures in defiance of his mother's wishes, since Bertrando, an ex-priest, and Silvio Spaventa, who had offended Croce's father, were barely on speaking terms with Croce's parents. Bertrando never knew that the young Croce had listened to his lectures. By the time of the earthquake, the famous Hegelian philosopher had died. Consequently, Silvio felt obligated to assume responsibility for the education of the young orphans. As a parent substitute, he played an important role in the development of both boys. He also provided a severe but passionately moral and political model. However, Silvio, who became their tutor in logic, could not replace a lost mother's warmth and love. The political atmosphere of the Spaventa household felt alien to Croce, who was accustomed to the serenity of village life.

Grief, Mourning, and Reparation

For two years, Croce grieved over his loss, years that he described as "my most painful and melancholy" ones. "This was the only period when often by night . . . I had a strong desire to not awaken in the morning. Even thoughts of suicide arose before me."[14] A wish to join the dead frequently occurs in such survivors.[15] Croce recorded many reasons for his melancholy:

> Various causes contributed to this depression: the heart-rending deaths of my parents and sister; the state of my health; my adolescent crisis; the loss of religious faith followed by the need for a new vision of the universe which I had not succeeded in finding; the pessimistic political am-

bience in the home of my uncle Spaventa; the complete lack of friends and relations of my youth; the long distance from Naples to which memories of family and infancy tied me; the uncertainty regarding my studies, since I was divided between a curiosity for erudition and bibliophily, and a philosophic interest that stimulated me to provide myself with a reason for every thing, but was accompanied by a diffidence which tended to limit me to mere erudition; the need in short for discipline and the guidance of others, accompanied by an impatience with any discipline and by a precocious critical spirit.[16]

Eventually Croce would repeat his childhood trauma by symbolically burying himself in the past, only to discover a new form of liberty, which would become a guiding precept in all of his literary, historical, and philosophical investigations. As late as 1942 he wrote: "A man whose mind is so religiously disposed . . . fixes his thoughts on moral history where is unfolded the drama which also goes on in himself, and where throughout the centuries he meets his fathers and brothers, who loved liberty as he does, and like him knew how to work and suffer for her."[17]

In the compiling of his "bricks" or *mattoni* (a term that Italian scholars used to describe the more than seventy volumes, which had bindings of a burnt sienna color),[18] Croce sought to reconcile himself with the reality of his early tragedy. His task became, in his own terms, one of distinguishing between what was living (*vivo*) and what was dead (*morto*) in past philosophical theories. The emotional privation from his terrible loss may well have provided him with a spur toward writing, thinking, and polemicizing.

When Croce was asked to write his autobiography, he replied: "the chronicle of my life lies entirely in the chronology and bibliography of my literary work."[19] This response was consistent with his refusal to engage in psychological or psychoanalytic explanations and interpretations of events. Indeed, he did not believe in unconscious determinants of conscious behavior. Psychoanalytically, Croce's denial could be termed a defense mechanism. For him, however, unconscious motives and underlying causes as such did not form the subject matter of aesthetic or philosophic work. His omission of these factors in his literary critiques has prompted criticism about Croce's aridity and "inhuman" treatment of poets and thinkers. The style of Croce's own autobiographical sketch provoked Middleton Murray to ask: "Can it be that there is a fundamental aridity in the Philosopher of the Spirit?"[20] This query seems especially ironic in the light of Croce's view that the "subject matter" of art and even the subject of philosophic judgment consisted of intuitional and representational feeling.

Croce and Hegel

In many ways a conventional young man, Croce nonetheless exhibited an appetite for unconventional ideas—an appetite now whetted by guests of Silvio Spaventa. They included deputies, professors, and journalists who engaged in heated debates about juridical and political problems. Spaventa was a Hegelian defender of historicism and evolutionist theories. He continued to provide an inspiring model and inevitably Croce's thought became influenced by his surrogate father's views. Later, however, Croce admitted that his contact with Hegel, apart from his intellectual ambience (which may have exercised a considerable if indirect influence upon him) did not begin by way of Neapolitan Hegelianism and the Spaventas. In fact, while living at Silvio's house, Croce tried to read Bertrando's works but became alienated from Hegel. Only subsequently, through his Marxist readings and contacts with the anti-Hegelian Antonio Labriola, was Croce introduced to Hegel's philosophy.[21] For some time he would be wary of what he felt to be the a priori and dogmatic elements in the German philosopher's views. Still later Croce began to deal with the Hegelian system more directly through his contact with Giovanni Gentile, who provided a more flexible interpretation than had the Spaventas.[22]

In 1904 Croce wrote an essay called "*Siamo noi hegeliani?*" (Are we Hegelians?) in response to critics who described the direction of his journal, *La critica: Rivista di letteratura, storia e filosofia*, as Hegelian or neo-Hegelian.[23] Here, as in his 1903 "*Il programma della 'critica'*"[24] (The program of *La critica*), he wished to indicate an antimetaphysical approach and thus preferred to call his new idealism a critical or realistic one. But not until 1905 did Croce actually read Hegel and put aside interpretations derived from his commentators. Significantly, Croce described this effort as "plunging into myself." [25] Out of his investigations came his 1906 essay, *"Ciò che è vivo e ciò che è morto della filosofia di Hegel"* [26] (What is living and what is dead of Hegel's philosophy), which, greatly developed, was published in 1907 as a book under the same title. [27]

Despite Croce's subsequent criticism of the Hegelian system, he remained strongly influenced by the German philosopher's ideas. Late in his career, in *My Philosophy,* Croce wrote that he felt distress over Hegel and that he "could live neither with him nor without him." [28] Cecil Sprigge, longtime friend, translator, and biographer of Croce, has commented "that the torments and consolations of love, in the literal sense, entered somehow into the matter, is perhaps not unfairly inferred from Croce's old-age fantasy on the life of Hegel, permeated, one feels, with self-portraiture, and suggesting with an admirable delicacy the reflections of early love in Hegel's work." [29] Hegelian notions did occur throughout Croce's writings. For instance, he named certain concepts "concrete-universals" (*"l'universale-concreto"*) as Hegel had done, to indicate that unity between the ideal and real, the eternal and historical which expressed the nature of a pure concept or category.

Spaventa enrolled Croce in a course of jurisprudence at the University of Rome with the thought that he would become a diplomat. But the only lectures that Croce avidly followed were those given by Antonio Labriola, professor of moral philosophy and former student of Bertrando Spaventa. [30] Croce's "anguished need to reformulate a faith in life, its goals, and its duties were unexpectedly fulfilled by Labriola," [31] a friend and visitor of the Spaventa household. During his youth Labriola had been a Herbartian who believed in transcendent values. By 1885, however, he was a Marxist who had been in correspondence with Engels and many leaders of international socialism. [32] It was at this time, through Labriola's lectures, that Croce was introduced to the discipline of economics. To Labriola's lectures and to De Sanctis's work Croce attributed the fact that he never became a positivist or an empiricist—views that were fashionable during that period. He spent many hours in research, often poorly organized, in the Casanatense library; eventually Croce learned the technique of bibliographic work.

"History Subsumed under the General Concept of Art"

In 1885, before completion of his formal education, Croce returned to Naples, where, although not yet twenty years old, he began administering his family estates—a task assumed by his brother in 1890, when he left military service to join Benedetto. From 1886 to 1891 along with his managerial projects Croce was absorbed in research on the history of his city and its culture. Out of these archival studies came a number of essays, some of which were published subsequently in a book on the Neapolitan Revolution in 1799. He also began a review called *Napoli nobilissima,* which among other topics treated the history of art. Although Croce was highly praised for these studies, he was left upon their completion with feelings of satiety and disgust. It was at that time that Croce resolved to accomplish something "more serious" and more "inward."[33] Thus his next project was to be a national (not municipal) history of the spiritual (not merely political) life of Italy from the time of the Renaissance. The subject matter and magnitude of his new task prompted Croce to investigate the nature of history and knowledge. Accordingly he read many books by Italian and German authors on these topics, and for the first time Croce studied Giambattista Vico's *Scienza nuova.* Years earlier, while attending the *liceo,* Croce had read De Sanctis's theory of literary criticism, and from that time forward he had been interested in aesthetics. So now it was natural for him to inquire about the relations between art and history. His investigations culminated in a philosophic essay entitled *"La storia ridotta sotto il concetto generale dell'arte"* (History subsumed under the general concept of art).[34] This work had been stimulated by the nineteenth-century positivistic view of history as a natural science—a conception that Croce, although opposed to metaphysics, had rejected. For him neither history nor philosophy belonged to Herbert Spencer's "positive science." Later Croce was to consider positivism in terms of a corrective reaction to idealistic metaphysics. At this time he also wanted to determine the *raison d'être* for his intense historical investigations.

The 1893 essay that delineated the relations between history and art was for Croce "like a revelation by himself about himself" (*"come una rivelazione di me a me stesso"*).[35] A reciprocal and dialectical rapport between history and theory continued to occur throughout Croce's later writings. A solid historical base thus provided fertile ground for his theoretical essays. The richness of such a foundation, however, presented readers with mixed results. The contingency, complexity, and ever-changing character of the past at times rendered Croce's theories unclear, ambiguous, and inconsistent. In subsequent chapters I hope to clarify some of these problems and to determine what remains alive— to borrow his own expression—in the Crocean philosophy.

Croce and Marx

In 1895 Croce's former professor at the University of Rome, Antonio Labriola, who had publically declared himself a socialist, sought help from his student for publication of his essays on Karl Marx. By this time, however, Croce was becoming disenchanted with Marxism.[36] His intense study of Marx's work led to debates with Vilfredo Pareto, the economist and sociologist. During their arguments Croce deduced that the two men were pursuing two quite different goals. Whereas Croce, the humanist, was interested in developing a phenomenology of the human spirit, Pareto, the scientist, was investigating uniformities present in the phenomena of production and exchange. As a result of his exchanges with Pareto, Croce proposed that economic activity consisted of an exercise of will, which acted independently of moral choice. Indeed throughout his life Croce maintained that the "economic fact is the practical activity of man, independent of any moral or immoral direction."[37] For him the economic act was moreover a universal one in the sense that it was coequal with (neither superior nor inferior to) the ethical, logical, and aesthetic expressions of human consciousness.

Thus man was not fundamentally simply an economic animal, as Marx had held; he was also moral, philosophical, and aesthetic. Subsequently Croce came to describe economic activity as a kind of amoral vitality that as such was not duty bound. He eventually would completely work through and transcend his early fascination with Marxism—never to return to his youthful infatuations with metaphysical realism and Marxist materialism. In 1900 he published *Materialismo storico ed economia marxistica* (later translated as *Historical Materialism and the Economics of Karl Marx*),[38] which he later considered to be his definitive work on Marx. To quote Croce himself:

> I think that I have shown clearly enough that Marx, while he may have successfully dressed up the Idea of Hegel in a materialistic or rather an economic garb, introduced no speculative or logical improvement into the Hegelian system whatever. He accepted in its entirety, the inferior and antiquated part of that system, of theological origin, and practically ignored the rest of it. In other words he accepted just what modern philosophic criticism, on the strength of over a century of Hegelian controversies and mental experiments, has rejected.[39]

Many years later, Antonio Gramsci, a founder of the Italian Communist party, would insist that a thorough reading and working through of Croce's philosophy was essential to a good Communist education.[40] Followers of Gramsci have argued that Croce's late emphasis upon the concept of vitality meant that he came to believe that the economic impulse was fundamental to all human behavior. (Croce had defined such an impulse as one's will of an immediate goal.) In my opinion, however, a careful reading of Croce's work will not justify this interpretation. Eventually he would stress the interrelatedness of theoretical and practical activities. Yet for Croce, in their logical order of dependency, praxis always followed upon theory, and intuitional rather than economic expression remained relatively autonomous. Gramsci's followers have neglected, moreover, the fact that Croce's humanism was both antimetaphysical and anti-utopian. "Progress," if understood in Marx's sense of that term, was never a Crocean concept of historical interpretation. Indeed, one who looks for a precursor of contemporary Marxism in Italy should give serious consideration to Giovanni Gentile's revised attitude toward it and to his conception of a "humanism of labor." One does not want to push this interpretation too far, but it is tempting to speculate on the extent to which present-day Italian Marxism has its theoretic roots in the philosophy of the doctrinaire spokesman for the Fascist regime.

La critica *and Giovanni Gentile*

In November 1902, Croce and his younger collaborator, the Sicilian philosopher Giovanni Gentile, announced the publication of *La critica,* to be issued every two months. This journal was to promote a widespread reawakening of philosophic spirit, an awareness of *humanitas.* The philosophic position presupposed therein Croce labeled as a new idealism (*l'idealismo nuovo*), critical idealism or idealistic realism, which advocated an antimetaphysical and methodological approach to literary criticism, history, and philosophy. Gentile evaluated, author by author, the Italian philosophic work of the prior half-century, whereas Croce criticized the general literature of Italy from its unification. There are various and even divergent interpretations as to which of the philosophers exerted the greater influence on the other.[41] Clearly Croce and Gentile were in accord in their struggle against positivism and empiricism, as well as in their desire to develop further a humanistic tradition, which they saw in the relations between Vico, Kant, and Hegel among others. Both men held that philosophy was not an encyclopedia of the natural sciences, but an "autonomous science of values, that is, a science of the human spirit."[42] Their position implied a shift of interest from the world of nature to the world of humanity and in this respect represented a reaction against positivism—especially the work of Herbert Spencer, Roberto Ardigò, and Cesare Lombroso.

The outlines of the Crocean philosophy were evident by the time of their collaboration or soon thereafter, but the development of Gentile's system took a direction quite different from Croce's philosophy. According to Gentile, thought and will became merged, and ethical activity was fundamental to every other expression of the human spirit. For Croce, however, theory and philosophy remained independent of praxis and politics. The relative autonomy of theory provided the philosophic justification for Croce's steadfast belief in freedom of speech and the grounds for his criticism of Fascist censorship. As time passed the two philosophers, Gentile and Croce, who differed in political ideology and temperament, continued to develop divergent lines of thought. In 1920, Gentile founded a new review, *Giornale critico della filosofia italiana*. Cecil Sprigge believed that the breach reached its peak in 1913 with the publication of "Discussion between Philosophic Friends."[43] But subsequently H. S. Harris has argued that their relationship was not severed completely, since the second edition of Gentile's *Teoria generale dello spirito come atto puro* (1918, translated as *Theory of Mind as Pure Act* [1922]),[44] was dedicated to Croce. And in 1921, Croce's introduction to the English translation of Gentile's *The Reform of Education*[45] demonstrated, to Harris's mind at least, the divergent yet complementary tenets present in their thought.[46]

The Foundations of the Crocean Philosophy

The same year Croce started *La critica* saw the publication of his first major work on aesthetics, *Estetica come scienza dell'espressione e linguistica generale* (1902; translated as *Aesthetic as Science of Expression and General Linguistic* [1902, 1922]).[47] Here he argued for the autonomy of art as distinguished from history and philosophy. Three additional volumes— on logic, economics and ethics, and historiography—followed.[48] These four books purported to give a complete inventory of the activities of the human spirit. Works on Vico and Hegel also were published,[49] and Croce's eminence as a philosopher became recognized by the conferment of a life senatorship in 1910.

In 1904, Croce became an adviser to the publisher Laterza and Sons of Bari. By means of his trenchant essays in *La critica,* and his collaboration with Laterza, Croce slowly educated his countrymen. His criticism, in fact, could ruin or secure the careers of aspiring young writers, historians, and philosophers. In "Some Personal Recollections," Professor Guido Calogero recalled his reactions to Croce's comments: "I think that the most wonderful love letter could not have given me greater pleasure, even at a time when I had not received any." Croce's "favorable judgment," Calogero continued, "was eagerly sought as a sort of knightly investiture on the field of literary and philosophical criticism."[50]

Minister of Education

In 1920, Giovanni Giolitti (a major figure in the Italian parliaments of 1900–15) became prime minister of Italy. He asked Croce to accept the post of minister of education. Croce accepted but unfortunately his tenure lasted only a year. Giolitti was followed by Mussolini, who selected Gentile as the new minister of education. In 1922, when the Fascist march on Rome shook the foundations of Italian life, Croce entertained high hopes that Mussolini might extend civil liberties along with social order in Italy. According to Dr. Manlio Brosio, former Italian ambassador to England, "Some people have blamed Croce for his attitude during the early days of Fascism, saying that he supported the regime between 1922 and 1924. Actually, his hope was that Fascism would prove only a transitory phenomenon, and in that sense a salutary one. In those first years he held the illusion that Fascism would fade of itself, and thus leave the way open for a more serious and better regulated liberal regime."[51] Croce's commendation to R. G. Collingwood revealed that in 1922 Douglas Ainslie's admiration of Mussolini, along with his protestations that although he translated Croce's work he did not share his ideas, caused Croce to ask Collingwood to translate his *Storia d'Italia dal 1871 al 1915* (1928). Yet as late as 1924 and even after the Matteotti murder, Croce voted for a motion of confidence in the government. Apparently, he still believed that Mussolini could be controlled and eventually dispatched when the Fascist leader became no longer useful.

The "Contromanifesto"

Finally, in 1925, much to Mussolini's sorrow, Croce began to speak out against what had become a dictatorship of the right. Mussolini subsequently invited Croce himself to become minister of education and later offered him a position in the Italian Academy. On both occasions Croce declined Mussolini's invitation. In the same year, Gentile's signature on the "Manifesto of Fascist Intellectuals" publicly marked the end of his long friendship with Croce. Croce then wrote his "Contromanifesto," signed by other distinguished scholars, who rejected Gentile's claim that Fascism possessed a cultural mission. Consistent with the Crocean view of the relations among forms of conscious expression, the "Contromanifesto" maintained that art was autonomous and should not be subordinated to political goals. It described Fascism as "an incoherent and bizarre mixture of appeals to authority and demagogy, of professions of reverence for the laws, ultramodern concepts and moth-eaten bric-à-brac, absolutism and Bolshevism, unbelief and toadying to the Catholic church, flight from culture and sterile reachings towards a culture without a basis, mystical languors and cynicism." [52] Gentile became the spokesman for the Fascist government and Croce its outspoken opponent. His was the only speech against the Lateran Pacts of 1929, which secured a reconciliation of the Roman church with the Kingdom of Italy and which restored a token territorial sovereignty to the Pope. Although Mussolini exercised control over the press, for about twenty years Croce was able to oppose *Il Duce* effectively from the platform of *La critica*. Indeed from 1903 to 1943, *La critica* greatly benefited from Croce's active correspondence with Italians and non-Italians, among the latter Albert Einstein, Thomas Mann, André Gide, and Julius von Schlosser. During this period, Croce also traveled often, both in Italy and abroad, where he met with other anti-Fascists such as Carlo Sforza, Carlo Rosselli, Alberto Tarchiani, Lionello Venturi, and Giuseppe Saragat. Feo wrote that during the twenty years of Fascism, Croce became little more than an exile in his own country. Although not banned, his works were discreetly displayed on the back shelves of libraries and bookstores, his books were removed from scholastic curricula and replaced by those of Gentile. Croce's name was omitted from leading newspapers, yet *La critica* was neither censored nor suppressed. And until 1933, its subscribers included universities and secondary schools.

As time passed, it became dangerous to be seen with Croce, and visitors were infrequent to his Palazzo Filomarino in Naples. Although he was too powerful to be imprisoned along with the other anti-Fascist intellectuals and professors whom Mussolini incarcerated, he lived under constant surveillance by the police. Indeed, one year after he (along with Giovanni Amendola, Francesco Ruffini, Roberto Bracco, and others) had replied to the Fascist intellectuals with an anti-Fascist manifesto, his palazzo was invaded by a squad of Blackshirts. Croce himself emphasized the damage caused by the "nocturnal assault on his library by Fascist roughs." [53] Mussolini was criticized for spending over a quarter of a million lire on Croce's surveillance, and he ordered it stopped. [54] Soon thereafter Croce joined the Italian Liberal party, which at that time barely existed.

According to Croce, "liberty" was a directive concept for historical narrative as well as humankind. His major works on history completed during the Fascist regime clearly illustrated the importance that he gave to this concept—one doubtless reinforced by restrictions upon personal and political freedom that occurred during this period. Even social justice, for Croce, played a role subordinate to political freedom. Guido Calogero described a heated discussion that took place during World War II: Croce "objected to the tenet that social justice was no less essential to political freedom than political freedom was to social justice. From the philosophical point of view, he maintained that freedom could never be subordinated to any other idea or ideal. . . . Theoretically, he was not against social reforms; practically, he feared their being adopted in a hurry, and insisted that Italy's first need was the restoration of political freedom and constitutional life." [55]

The Collapse of Fascism: Crocean Liberalism

Upon the collapse of Fascism with Marshal Pietro Badoglio's Palace Revolution in 1943, Crocean liberalism became prominent among the competing political parties, and Croce himself participated in the formation of the new post–World War II government. Some would say that he served more as an inspiration and symbol than as a creator of actual policy, since Croce still believed in the monarchal institution. Eventually, however, he became disillusioned with King Victor Emmanuel III and demanded his abdication. The old monarch not only had sought to recapture his earlier political power; he also tried to reestablish a disguised type of semi-Fascism under liberal forms. Croce countered the king's attempt and urged the formation of a regency to rule in the name of the regent Prince Humbert, the king's son. This proposal was unsuccessful, but eventually the king was persuaded to retire.

At Salerno during April 1944, Croce became a minister without portfolio of the new democratic government of Italy; in July, he joined the cabinet formed by Ivanoe Bonomi. Now eighty years old, Croce refused the suggestion that he seek election to become the provisional head of the Italian state. From 1944 to 1947, even after Croce had left the government, he remained president of the Liberal party, an office that he had assumed subsequent to the liberation of Italy. In this way he participated in political activities after the fall of Mussolini and during the reconstruction of contemporary Italy. He thus remained true to his belief that "no man could escape politics, lest politics would disturb him in the very heart of his private life."[56]

Quaderni della "Critica"

In 1943 the British military occupied the publishing offices at Bari, and *La critica* was succeeded by the *Quaderni della "Critica."*[57] Unlike *La critica,* wherein Croce's voice dominated Italian culture to an extent not seen in any other European country, the *Quaderni* had to contend with a variety of views deriving from the Resistance cultural legacy— all struggling for power. Young critical intellectuals felt that Croce's humanistic liberalism was too elitist, traditional, and conservative to lead the emergence of Italy's "New Culture." In fact Croce did hold that a task of the intellectual elite was to educate the masses, as *La critica* had tried to accomplish for so many decades. Croce's position as a southerner, as the leader of the more traditional, less industrialized, and backward part of Italy, as the head of the conservative Liberal party, and as a philosophic idealist rather than a materialist, all led people to affirm moreover that he was a defender of the status quo. Indeed we have seen that he supported the institution of the monarchy and the propertied classes. The political left began to attack Croce's views. In 1944 Palmiro Togliatti's Communist journal *Rinascita* published some parts of Gramsci's prison correspondence, which were quite critical of the Crocean philosophy.[58] Gramsci saw the role of the intellectual as far more political and activist than had Croce. Ironically the Marxist philosophy that Croce thought he had laid to rest in the preceding century not only would replace Croce's philosophic idealism and political liberalism, but would also claim the former as its legitimate predecessor.

In 1946, six years before his death, Croce founded and endowed his vast private library in the Palazzo Filomarino, as a school of historical studies for postgraduates.

We may infer from this biographical sketch that Croce was a man of wide interests and talents that provided the content for his philosophy of the human spirit. He was not only a contemplative person, a profound scholar who buried himself in his study and wrote learned books on many different studies. Croce also engaged vigorously in the reform of Italian politics and education. Indeed there was no aspect of Italian life in which Croce's name did not appear, even to the final disposition of Mussolini's papers. My concern, however, is not with Croce's political or social activities, nor even with his philosophy of the practical sphere of human endeavors—the economic, political, and ethical as Croce defined them. Instead in the chapters that follow I treat the philosophical conceptions of truth, error, and objectivity, since it was in that realm where Croce made a major contribution to contemporary philosophic thought. But prior to any discussion of these topics, let us outline the Crocean philosophy, so that we can understand how they arose within the context of Croce's thought.

2

An Outline of the Crocean Philosophy

Croce believed that his philosophy continued a tradition of European rational speculation. He interpreted his task, accordingly, as one of distinguishing between what is "living" or true, and what is "dead" or false in the history of philosophy. What then for Croce formed the subject matter of philosophic inquiry? And what were its results? The philosopher was not to treat substantive issues, whether metaphysical or ontological. Croce's orientation was indeed antimetaphysical in the sense that he wanted to eliminate transcendent elements from his atheistic, humanistic philosophy. The essence of philosophy lay not in a doctrine of abstract unchanging truths but in getting "rid of the pretence or illusion that a philosopher's work or 'system' is a self-completed revelation of the so-called 'mystery of reality'." [1]

Philosophy as an Open-Ended Enterprise

For Croce there was no final philosophy because reality itself was always changing. Provisional answers to philosophic questions stimulated new problems for the inquiring mind. Answers as well as problems were conditioned by the historical contexts in which they arose. In this respect Crocean thought continued the tradition of European nineteenth-century historicism. In *My Philosophy* Croce stated that "the very thing I was deliberately denying was the indivisible unity of philosophic systems. Apart from prejudice, I clearly saw behind the apparent unity a series or complex of particular problems, some successfully solved and others not, systematised up to a point, but only in provisional systems, which always must be and always are open to reconsideration in the light of later experience and later inevitable problems arising by historical necessity."[2] Croce's concept of philosophy as an open-ended enterprise, not itself subject to revision, will allow us to interpret major theoretical changes in his views.

The Subject Matter and Method of Philosophy

What then was the province of philosophic thought? The philosopher was to explore the activities of thought and will. These theoretical and practical expressions of imagination, thought, action, and morality manifested themselves as perennial a priori categories, sometimes called concrete-universals or pure concepts—aesthetic, logical, economic, and ethical. The discovery and delineation of categories as they occurred throughout history constituted Croce's *filosofia dello spirito,* by which he meant a philosophy of the human spirit. Croce's concept of *lo spirito* is a difficult one for Americans, especially Anglo-Saxons, to understand and needs clarification. I hope that by emphasizing that the roots of Crocean phenomenology lay in his post-Kantian gnoseology, his humanistic concept of spirit will become clear.

What was the method, so characteristic of Croce's philosophy? His approach was one of self-examination, which consisted of a kind of introspective inspection of consciousness. By "introspection," Croce did not mean anything resembling psychoanalytic inquiry. He denied the existence of an unconscious mind and proposed that the self became revealed in one's conscious creative acts. For him even the "true biography of a person" lay in the "history of his work or of his action."[3] Croce displayed no interest in what might remain behind or beyond these events. And he clearly illustrated his aversion to any such possibility in his own biographical sketch, where he discussed the development of his personal philosophy exclusively in relation to its historical influences—

understood not in a private sense, but as determinants of an ongoing process. Contributions to his thought included the works of Vico, Kant, and Hegel. Nor did the Crocean self-examination issue in confession of emotion, which for him would have amounted to poetry. Rather, the philosopher was to develop a self-awareness that revealed theoretical (cognitive) and practical (volitional) forms of conscious expression.[4]

Croce's Speculative Method

Croce labeled his method "speculative," by which he meant that mind was to become cognizant of its own functions and structures. His description, however, should not be understood as implying some form of traditional metaphysic. By calling his approach "speculative," Croce wished to distinguish it especially from forms of empiricism. The fundamental tenets of his philosophy, thus, did not amount to empirical claims, since Croce's introspective method purported to discover categories and concepts not derived a posteriori and by induction. Philosophy was to make explicit a priori categories of judgment used in historical narrative. This is what Croce had in mind when he described philosophy as the "methodological moment of historical narrative." Neither history nor philosophy occurred without the other. On the one hand, historical narrative required categorial interpretation. On the other, philosophic categories inevitably presented themselves in historical contexts and thereby provided a framework in terms of which events and subjects were to be interpreted. In subsequent chapters I argue that Croce's exclusively nonempirical methodology did not account for all types of true judgment; nor did it satisfactorily determine objective narrative.

Philosophy and "Experience"

Although Croce disavowed the use of induction as a way of gaining genuine knowledge, he did claim that philosophy was always to be subject to the test of "experience" and must be revised accordingly. How can we interpret, within the Crocean framework, this apparent inconsistency between speculative method and an appeal to "experience"? "Experience," according to Croce, included the results of his phenomenological, autocritical inventory of the human spirit. However, for the English or American reader, who might associate "experience" with empiricism, perhaps "consciousness" or "conscious expression" would better indicate Croce's meaning. And as I have suggested, for him philosophy itself possessed an expansive, changing character, whereas man's logical, conceptual mode of apprehending the world remained perennial. Philosophies were thus emendable, corrigible, and subject to autocritical scrutiny, although the philosophic process itself was "eternal."

The same point applied to Croce's own philosophy, inasmuch as a repeated assimilation and transcendence came to characterize his thought. Even he was aware that subsequent philosophers would discard and surpass his ideas, just as in the past he had developed beyond what he had formerly held to be true. Croce had prophesied accordingly that his own thought would be superseded by the "*unda quae supervenit undam,* by the growth and widening of the human spirit."[5] Whether the tension between the perennial and the particular in Croce's concept of philosophy and within the concrete-universal itself amounted to an unresolved ambiguity suggests questions to be raised subsequently. Here I wish only to introduce the reader to this important problem. If there is an explanation of the paradoxical nature of the Crocean conception of the concept, it will lie in the logical synthetic a priori activity of the human spirit.

Intuitional Cognition

Philosophers who initiated their speculations by examining consciousness have attempted to discover the basic or "primitive" elements present in cognition. Croce, for one, described such expressions of consciousness as "intuitions."[6] What were these intuitions that remained implicitly and explicitly present in our every thought, as well as in the most simple conscious awareness? The Crocean intuitions were impressions (*impressioni*) and expressions of feelings (*sentimenti*).[7] The expressive process involved making more or less clear to one's self what one's awarenesses were. To have been expressed intuitionally was tantamount to becoming an *object* (image or feeling) for consciousness. Croce described the process of expression thus as one of "objectification." In addition, intuitions were not to be described in abstraction from their theoretic cognitive process; nor was the intuitional process to be considered as divorced from intuition itself. During their occurrence, intuitions and their expressions were indistinguishable from one another. At a later moment (when we judged our awareness), we could differentiate our intuitional *act* of apprehending an object from its "image" (*imago*) or expression in imagination. Croce held that this act of mind that created a synthesis among feelings and also provided the sine qua non for knowledge was an a priori one. It issued from a transcendental condition for intuition that Croce likened to "Kant's synthesizing activity of spirit: a concept, well recognized as not psychological in the sense of an empirical science, but as serving to establish the profound distinction between philosophy of the spirit and [empirical] psychology."[8] Unlike Kant's *Anschauung* of the sensible manifold, however, Crocean intuition was not apprehended under the a priori forms of sensibility, space and time. To quote Croce on this point: "We have intuitions without space and without time: the colour of a sky, the colour of a feeling, a cry of pain and an effort of will, objectified in consciousness: these are intuitions which we possess, and with their making space and time have nothing to do."[9]

Intuition as Feeling

Intuitional feelings were not mere appearances. What we usually considered invisible nonmaterial data—for example, feelings, emotions, states of mind—became the "matter" of what was immediately presented to us. Nevertheless we did express these intuitions in colors, words (written or spoken), and musical notes, which for Croce amounted to conscious, nonconceptual cognitions in the mind of the agent who expressed them. He described us as "intuitionally aware" during the act of regarding our surroundings while not judging them. While looking at a silver candlestick, for example, I noticed its rose-colored candle. The ridges cut in its wax made a spiral pattern ending a little below the wick. The gleam of the holder contrasted with the matte rosy hue of the candle, which, leaning slightly, formed an angle with its vertical support. Concepts such as "reality," "existence," "truth," or "beauty" were not explicitly present during these observations. We may thus contemplate objects or events without judging them.

Nor should we confuse intuitions with irrational volitions or passive impressions. The former were active and "objectified" when we simultaneously apprehended and expressed them, while the latter remained unsynthesized or simple sensations merely juxtaposed to one another. Such feelings expressed an aggregate, a nonorganic association, when they were "put together for fun or business or for some other practical end."[10] In this case, consciousness aggregated, assembled, and associated images as in a jigsaw puzzle but did not synthesize them into an organic unity that would have required a powerful, dominant image.[11] Croce claimed that among the many examples of the mechanical combining of images, some occurred in *King Lear,* wherein

> the adventures of Gloucester and his sons inserted into those of Lear and his children are not completely satisfying. Perhaps this is due to the overly realistic element that these events introduce in the fable of the play; or because the scenes create a multilevel parallelism . . . that possibly stemmed from theatrical needs of complication and suspension, rather than from moral intent to emphasize horror at ingratitude.[12]

This passage suggests how Croce differentiated between the *immaginazione* that loosely associated images and the creatively functioning *fantasia,* a distinction not present in the first English translation of his 1902 *Estetica.*[13] Croce's concepts of the rearranging process of fancy and the creative imagination were akin to Coleridge's "fancy," which worked with fixities and definites, and to the transforming activity of "aesthetic imagination" requisite for metaphor and art.

The Crocean Concept

So far, we have considered the Crocean view of conscious cognitive expression, devoid of judgments about reality or unreality and about truth or falsehood. But our treatment needs to be supplemented, since intuitions alone cannot account for the range of human cognitive activities. What were the relations between intuition and concept? What was the nature of a concept or category? When we moved from *particular* intuition to *universal* concept, we passed from fantasy to reality. Feelings became transformed into universals by a creative, synthetic a priori act of mind. Pure intuition could occur, but cognitive reality usually included concepts. And although intuitions need not include concepts, the expression of concepts required intuitions. The relation of concept to intuition was accordingly asymmetrical, and the passage that follows gives us one of Croce's illustrations of this point:

> the spirit is thus conceived as consisting of four moments or degrees, disposed in such a way that the theoretical activity is to the practical as the first theoretical degree is to the second theoretical, and the first practical degree to the second practical. the four moments imply one another regressively by their concreteness. The concept cannot exist without expression, the useful without both and morality without the three preceding degrees. If the aesthetic fact is in a certain sense alone independent while the others are more or less dependent, then the logical is the least dependent and the moral will the most. [14]

Like intuition, the philosophic concept was also supposed to be "pure." By this adjective, Croce meant a universal that originated from the theoretical (cognitive) and not practical (volitional) activity of consciousness. He called the empirical and abstract representations issuing from the latter "pseudoconcepts" (*pseudoconcetti*).

Commentators have differentiated among principal categories of art, philosophy, the useful, and the ethical that represented the four fundamental activities of consciousness, and pure concepts or concrete-universals as, for example, "the beautiful" and "the lyrical," which pertained to art forms. Croce himself, however, apparently used the terms "category," "pure concept," and "concrete-universal" interchangeably. (Here I will follow Croce and hyphenate "concrete-universal" to indicate the organic unity between the two terms.) Any distinction between the Crocean categories, pure concepts, and concrete-universals should therefore be treated as hermeneutic or made for practical purposes, but not as corresponding to real differences existing within the realm of the theoretical. Indeed when the Italian philosopher was asked what were the differences between art, lyricality, and beauty, he replied that the terms were synonyms. I suppose that the same response could be given with regard to the relations between any of the other categories and their respective concepts. In subsequent discussion I likewise use the terms "category," "pure concept," and "concrete-universal" interchangeably.

Pure Concepts: Ultra- and Omnirepresentative

Croce described categories or pure concepts, such as the beautiful, the true, the useful, and the good, as "omnirepresentative" (*omnirappresentativi*). By this adjective, he meant that they were present—either implicitly in the sense of potentially or explicitly—in every aspect of reality. Conceptual expression, however, could not be exhausted in particular intuition since besides being omnirepresentative, it was "ultrarepresentative" (*ultrarappresentativa*) and superseded each aspect of the real. Although concepts expressed neither any one intuition nor merely a group of them, they nevertheless represented each and all intuitions at the same time. By the word "all" Croce meant possible as well as actual intuitions.

The Crocean concrete-universals were not metaphysical or ontological entities. Instead they were akin to Kant's synthetic a priori categories of the understanding and served an epistemological function. For it was Kant, Croce wrote, who had located the center of philosophic inquiry in the "gnoseology and philosophy of the spirit."[15] At times when Croce referred to such concrete-universals as art or logic, it was not clear whether he was describing the logical *process* of thought or one of its expressions. Frequently he meant both; indeed he asserted that the cognitive act consisted of its expression. As was the case with intuition, neither logical act nor conceptual expression was to be considered in abstraction from the other. This ambiguity of reference occurred not only in the case of logical activity and the concrete-universal, but also with intuition and its expression or image. Whereas in the former case the question of whether the Crocean concept possessed an ontological status might arise, in the latter the reader could be confused about the universality of the intuitive act and its aesthetic image. These are problems I shall address in the chapters that follow.

Although my discussion of the Crocean concept will suffice, I trust, to serve as an introduction, it remains incomplete, since a concept that did not express a judgment of a particular object was as unreal in the Crocean philosophy as an intention that was not an action. However, because Croce's theory of judgment is rather technical and complicated, it seems best to reserve treatment of it until chapter 4, where a detailed discussion is given. For this reason we will now inquire about the expressions of what Croce called the "practical" activities of consciousness. Humans willed and contemplated; they acted as well as thought. Thus according to Croce the life of one's spirit was as fully practical as it was theoretical.[16] The presence of will and its two forms, the economic and the ethical, were discoverable by the same philosophical self-examination that had revealed the cognitive activities of intuition and conception. Since theory and praxis along with their respective forms exhausted human activity, feeling or sentiment consisted of either aesthetic intuition or an expression of will.

Economic Volition and Empirical Pseudoconcepts

The first form of practical activity, the economic, was relatively autonomous within its sphere. Our desire for personal gain represented the most fundamental of the practical activities of spirit. Human non-universal will was not "immoral," but amoral. Expressions of "the practical" or "the vital impulse," as Croce called it in later works, included mind's creation of empirical pseudoconcepts. These terms amounted to classifications of objects for practical purposes of communication and induction. By means of class terms, a single name such as "cat" could invoke in our memory any number of images or representations of cats, or a word such as "college" could stimulate us to formulate a plan for the achievement of an expedient goal.

According to the Crocean philosophy, empirical pseudoconcepts did not comprise elements of knowledge, since in Croce's sense of ultra- and omnirepresentative, the extension of the classes to which they referred was limited by observation and stipulation of generic similarities and differences among objects. Such terms were not thus what Croce preferred to call "concepts." He referred to them as "pseudoconcepts" and contrasted them with the universals or pure concepts, which occurred solely in the sphere of the theoretical:

> For brevity's sake we shall call them [empirical class names] pseudoconcepts, and for the sake of clearness we shall call the true and proper concepts pure concepts. . . . The pseudoconcepts . . . are not concepts. They do not form a species of, nor do they compete with concepts (save when forcibly made to do so).[17]

Empirical terms were expressed in like statements. "The play *Hamlet* is a tragedy," for instance, was an empirical judgment for Croce, because its predicate was a class term and not a concrete-universal. Here the pseudoconcept "tragedy" resulted from observing and classifying according to characteristics, such as the hero's noble character, a fatal flaw that determined his undoing, his fall from eminence and power. These marks, although useful for categorizing, need not have qualified "tragedy." An objector might argue cogently that this genre could not occur within a Christian framework that offered the possibility of redemption, nor moreover in an age that lacked noble birth or heroes. The classes denoted by pseudoconcepts thus were arbitrarily created by mind's practical activity.

Empirical judgments, composed of representations and pseudoconcepts, were neither true nor false. Useful in the practical sense of classification and communication, they were a necessary consequence of the human wish to organize and to communicate experience. Pseudojudgments and the concepts they included were to be subjected not to the principle of contradiction, but instead to pragmatic criteria of convenience and utility. In short, such judgments could never be verified, but would be discarded when no longer practically indispensable. Thus in this way Croce came to distinguish sharply the philosophic from the empirical sciences. The latter resembled philosophy with respect to concreteness but lacked the universality yielded by the ultra- and omnirepresentative nature of the pure concepts that formed their subject matter.

Pure Concepts and Pseudoconcepts

Pseudoconcepts, according to Croce, depended on logical categories for their expression. What did he mean by his claim? The Crocean relationship between concrete-universal and empirical concept did not appear to be one of deduction, in the sense that, for example, the characteristics of a triangle could be deduced from its definition. Moreover, Croce himself denied that their order of dependency was one of simple temporal priority. Nor was the relationship one of "family resemblance" as in the case of a biological genus and species. Rather the pure concept "art" resulted from a *logical* activity of mind, whereas "tragedy," a pseudoconcept, issued from *practical* intent. Thus to say that pure concept was a necessary prerequisite for pseudoconcept meant that philosophical analysis of the acts of the human spirit would show that will was rational, that is, it required thought for its expression. Praxis was analyzable in terms of theory, whereas the reverse did not hold. Whether Croce's distinction between phenomenological and temporal priority was sustainable, or even whether Croce consistently maintained it, was questionable. There was no doubt, however, that it was an important one in Croce's philosophy. His task as he saw it was to preserve the autonomy of art and the freedom of philosophy from economic and political ideologies.

Abstract Pseudoconcepts

So far we have discussed generalizations from ordinary sense experience. What about the abstract notions of mathematics and geometry? These terms, although universal, possessed no representative content. As Croce put it: "There is no geometric triangle in reality because in reality there are no straight lines, nor right angles, nor sums of right angles, nor sums of angles equal to that of two right angles."[18] Such a sweeping statement needs further interpretation. But our outline of the Crocean philosophy is not the place. Chapter 4, which treats Croce's concept of the concept, will elaborate upon what he preferred to call "abstract" pseudoconcepts. Here we may characterize them briefly as being unlike the empirical ones with respect to their universality and lack of concreteness.

Ethical Expression: Will of a Universal Goal

We have discussed three activities and their expressions of the human spirit: the intuitional, the logical, and the economic. What about ethical activity? Like Kant, Croce held that our moral will sought what was universal; for Croce, however, it was also relative to the will of an immediate end ("economic activity"). Ethical volitions then became concrete in relation to utilitarian or economic activity. This meant that they occurred within historical limitations, for no moral expression could be devoid of them. Yet "the ethical," in its quest for political liberty, must also transcend cravings for short-lived satisfactions. Humans as "economic animals" willed their own existence: as moral beings, they were conscious of working for "the whole."[19]

Ethical volition was to "subdue" and "refashion" egoistic expression, "for human life is subject to this sole authority, which alone is competent to give the ultimate decision in moral conflicts by prescribing the action which may reconcile them."[20] Morality must, accordingly, work within the limitations of self-interest. It arose out of concrete circumstances whenever one transcended short-run self-interest in order to widen the degree of liberty that existed within a political state.

It was, moreover, human ethical aim that unified and vitalized the categories of spirit. After the 1902 *Estetica,* Croce relegated noncognitive feelings and sensations to what he called the "practical sphere" of consciousness (economic and ethical volitions), which supplied the material for the theoretic realm of intuition. The relations between these activities of mind suggested a circle. Ethical volitions of relatively universal goals became transformed into intuition and concept—which in turn formed the basis for self-interest and moral action. With emphasis upon the interdependency of our capacities to know and to will, Croce asserted that a man would not be moral, that is, he would not broaden his horizons beyond immediate needs and desires ("economic" volitions), if he could not imagine (intuit) and reason (conceptualize). Analogously, philosophizing required a sense of the poetic (intuition) and even moral intent.

The Unity of Conscious Expressions

Human consciousness, then, is truly unified insofar as each of its activities enhances and contributes to every other. In his *Defense of Poetry,* Croce metaphorically described expressions of mind as "paths" that "are not divergent nor even parallel, but join in a circle which is the rounded unity of the human spirit."[21] An individual, however, might remain "one-sided" and never experience all of his distinct capacities for aesthetic, philosophic, economic, and political or moral expression. These unfortunates are *"dimidiati viri"* (half-men). There is, for instance, the philosopher who does not carry out the practical obligations of his theory but "stands idle when he should be fulfilling his duties as a citizen and a soldier. There is the artistic genius who never effects the passage from the dreams of his poetry to philosophic thought and consistent action."[22] This "stunting" of life has undesirable consequences. The immoral philosopher doubts his intellectual capacities;

the creator of poetry degenerates into the stylist or purveyor of *belles lettres*.

Indeed, Croce's own life reflected a desire to surpass the boundaries of egoism. Italo De Feo has written of Croce's strong reluctance to accept the post of minister of education in 1920—a time when Italy was paralyzed by political strife. Croce, married and with children, was well settled in his *palazzo* in Naples. He wanted neither to enter political life nor to assume the burdens of bureaucracy. Feo quoted Croce's wife— upon perceiving his inner turmoil—as saying "If this be a duty to which you are called, you ought to accept it."[23] That evening Croce, leaving behind his beloved family and studies, departed for Rome.

We now see that for Croce, an ever-deepening understanding of the past became continuously integrated with the present. Throughout historical investigations, his Ariadne's thread, his guiding principle, was the moral element in human activity—the quest for liberty. Liberty was thus the directive concept for historical narrative and the moral ideal of humanity. Metaphorically translating Croce's childhood trauma into universal terms, we can say that the ethical goal of humankind lay in its struggle for greater political freedom within the confines of varying historical conditions. Croce, having lost his childhood world in the earthquake, drew upon the strengths of his early environment and created a universe for himself, only to transmute it during the evolution of his thought. As he put it: "A definite pronouncement of total truth would mean the burial of thought and all its doubts."[24]

My outline of Croce's *filosofia dello spirito* concludes with this brief discussion of the realm of the practical, which comprised the economic and ethical activity of the human spirit. Let us now focus our attention upon the development of Croce's theory of intuition so as to gain a better understanding of the subject of propositions and judgments.

3
The Sphere of the Aesthetic

The evolution of Benedetto Croce's theory of intuition itself reflected a "dialectical" movement of "thesis" and "transcendence" that characterized philosophy as he had defined it. Reciprocal relations among literature, history, and theory stimulated the development of the Crocean concept of intuition. At times, however, the richness of this "dialogue" yielded unfortunate consequences, and Croce's attempt to make explicit what was implicit in his experience as literary critic, historian, and philosopher rendered some of his concepts difficult to understand.[1] Croce's elaborations have suggested the following as yet unanswered questions, along with the possibly intractable nature of the problems involved in their solutions: What did Croce mean by "cosmic totality" when he attributed it to aesthetic expression? Were his further qualifications of the particular object of intuition incomprehensible? Or had Croce's embellishments represented a broadening and deepening, rather than a rejection, of his early view on intuition?

Occasionally, Croce's concept of intuition can be illustrated best by turning to passages drawn from its application in his literary criticism. Croce himself adopted this method of explicating his philosophical views, and its use remained consistent with his belief in a dynamic relationship between theory and practice. Nevertheless it may be difficult to synthesize his broad and impressionistic illustrations with specific concepts. The reader who can manage to do so, however, will gain a better understanding of the Crocean intuition.

Croce's most important statements about intuition occurred in his writings on aesthetics. These works included the *Primi saggi* (1919), *Estetica come scienza dell'espressione e linguistica generale* (1902; translated as *Aesthetic as Science of Expression and General Linguistic* [rev. ed. 1922]), *Breviario di estetica* (1913; translated as *Guide to Aesthetics* [1965]), and the essays *"L'intuizione pura e il carattere lirico dell'arte"* (1908; translated as "Pure Intuition and the Lyrical Character of Art" in the unrevised 1909 translation of the *Estetica*),[2] and *"Il carattere di totalità dell'espressione artistica"* (1918; translated as "The Totality of Artistic Expression" [1966]).[3] During his long and prolific career, Croce's concept of intuition continued to evolve. Let us take a close look at its major determinations before ascertaining whether they can be consistently absorbed within the framework of his theory.

"La storia ridotta sotto il concetto generale dell'arte"

The essays collected in the *Primi saggi,* published in 1919, present their reader with Croce's early philosophical thought on intuition, along with its relations to other kinds of expression—conceptual as well as noncognitive. These writings included an essay *"La storia ridotta sotto il concetto generale dell'arte"* (History subsumed under the general concept of art). Written seven years after Croce had left the University of Rome, it was read to the Accademia Pontaneana in March 1893. This important work had represented Croce's response to soul–searching for the *raison d'être* of his intense studies in the area of Neapolitan culture and history.

The intellectual background of *"La storia"* included Vico's distinction between metaphysics, which withdraws mind from sensations, and the poetic faculty, which should immerse mind in them: "Metaphysics elevates itself to the level of universals; the poetic faculty ought deeply to penetrate particular objects."[4] Vico's concepts of the noetic nature of art[5] and of the autonomy of aesthetic expression also must have influenced Croce either directly or indirectly through the philosophy of Francesco De Sanctis. They helped to form the thesis of *"La storia"*: intuition as art consisted of autonomous cognitive yet emotive expressions of the human spirit. While attending the *liceo,* Croce had studied De Sanctis's theory of literary criticism, some years before he would work through Vico's writings, and De Sanctis, strongly influenced by Vico's philosophy, had rejected Hegel's synthesis of art, philosophy, and religion. De Sanctis argued instead that art was autonomous. Croce wrote that he had gained this central idea also from De Sanctis, albeit in a crude form, "that art is not a work of reflection and logic, nor yet a product of skill, but pure and spontaneous imaginative form."[6] With regard to theory of history and cosmology, Croce considered his philosophy to be both anti-Hegelian and antimetaphysical. All of these views became reflected in his 1893 concept of history. Much later Croce recalled: "In 1892, the new philosophy of history and the old philosophy of art had stimulated my first philosophical essay. Subsequently, I was never able to abandon philosophic studies."[7]

History—Art or Science?

An important question frequently debated during the latter part of the nineteenth century—especially in Germany, but also in Italy and elsewhere on the Continent—asked: Is history an art or a science? Croce's essay of 1893 responded to this general question and to Pasquale Villari's 1891 article in *La nuova antologia,* which considered whether history was a science.[8] Croce's primary thesis was that history was neither an empirical nor an abstract science. Study of the past was to be included instead under the concept of art as *intuition* of *particular* objects. Croce's position expressed his own reply to the intellectual domination of the nineteenth-century positivists and evolutionists—especially to the work of Herbert Spencer. The Italian philosopher directed his arguments thus against those positivistic and scientific ideas that had infected much of late nineteenth-century historiography and theory of history. According to the philosophical materialists of that period, art, poetry, and beauty were sensuous pleasures. They needed to explain what for Croce amounted to expressions of the human spirit, in terms of psychological associations, habits, and inherited dispositional traits. For such philosophers the usual answer to the question raised above was that history is a science.[9]

Intuition as Cognitive Yet Emotive Expression

In opposition to utilitarian and behavioristic accounts, Croce asserted that aesthetic intuition was a cognitive yet emotive expression of the human spirit, not a turbid, obscure vibration of one's brain.[10] In addition, intuition was not to be confused with a state of idle passive awareness or daydreaming; rather, it issued from an active, creative and not merely reproductive expression of imagination. Some scholars have argued that until the publication of the *Breviaro di estetica* in 1913, or perhaps not even until after 1919, Croce ambiguously described intuition as being both active and passive.[11] A reason for this apparent confusion probably lies in the passive connotations implied by some of the synonyms, such as representation, impression, and contemplation, that Croce used for "intuition." It has been thought, moreover, that early in his career Croce supposed that mind was a kind of passive receptacle that simply reproduced impressions received from the "external world." Yet passages in *"La storia ridotto sotto il concetto generale dell'arte"*[12] and in subsequent writings, wherein Croce distinguished between the creative activity of the *fantasia* and the mechanical functioning of the *immaginazione* or fancy, suggest that the contrary was the case. Moreover, such an interpretation is not consistent with the Kantian and Hegelian influences upon Croce's philosophy, nor with his subsequent elaboration of the synthetic a priori activities of consciousness. So although some descriptions did emphasize the intuitional aspect of impression rather than expression, the ambiguity appears to be more verbal than substantive, since Croce described expression along with impression as integral to the *organic unity* of the intuitional process.

Intuition as Distinguished from Concept

Although Crocean intuition was to be considered cognitive, it was not so in a conceptual (*conoscenza intellettiva*)—that is, in a philosophical or scientific—sense. The subject matter of both philosophy and science consisted of general concepts, whereas that of art and history comprised unique individuals or particular objects, about which no generalization could be rendered.[13] (Subsequently Croce distinguished between "the individual," which served as subject of historical judgment, and "particular" as it described the object of intuition.) Croce illustrated the intuitive act by asking the reader to contemplate quite ordinary items— for example, a table, chair, desk, or tree. Each of these representations was particular and unique. Thus none could be deduced from a generalization. Inasmuch as art and history were *contemplative* of individuals, these disciplines did not investigate their causes. Scientific judgment, on the contrary, was not descriptive. It prescribed the behavior of objects according to law.

Croce and Baumgarten on Intuition

In the 1895 *"Illustrazione e discussioni"* included in the *Primi saggi,* Croce likened his concept of intuition to A. G. Baumgarten's *cognitio sensitiva* (affective cognition).[14] Nevertheless their views differed in important respects. The *cognitio sensitiva* yielded obscure ideas that were sensuous and emotive but *inferior* to the clear and distinct ideas of logic. Even though Croce recognized the poetic nature of intuition, he argued against positions that advocated either its inferior or superior status vis-à-vis conceptual reasoning. Accordingly, art as based upon intuition of particular images, and logic or philosophy, which treated concepts and their relations to one another, were to be considered on equal footing. In the Crocean view, sensuous representations of possible particulars also remained autonomous (that is, their occurrence depended on no other type of cognition), within the theoretic or cognitive sphere of human activity.

According to Baumgarten, art could represent intuitional cognition of what was moreover true and real. In Croce's view, *strictly speaking,* it did not express any such knowledge. Art represented instead possible *qua* possible or imaginary particulars (*"individuale immaginato o puramente possibile"*). Within the artist's aesthetic imagery, the outside world had not as yet emerged as false or real. By virtue of its creative nature, then, the realm of art remained more extensive than that of history, for art represented pure possibility, whereas history was to narrate what actually happened (*"Ciò ch'è realmente accaduto"*).[15]

Relations between Art and History

What then did Croce mean by "subsume" (*"ridotto sotto"*), when he argued that history was to be subsumed under the concept of art? He did not intend that history was to be reduced simply to art: the historian did not speculate about what might have been (Croce's definition of "the possible"), but described the real individual (*"individuale reale"*). He narrated what actually took place. Moreover, as we have seen, "subsume" did not denote a whole-to-part relationship with regard to the respective contents of history and art, since history was not to narrate possible objects, nor was art to express actual *qua* actual ones. Here Croce's point was that both disciplines represent particular (*"individuali"*) objects and not universal concepts or laws. Art and history depended on mind's intuitional rather than its conceptual activity.

To summarize: in opposition to the positivists' view that history was a natural science, Croce argued that knowledge of the past embraced cognition of individuals and not universals.[16] Consequently historical narrative could not form a science composed of empirical laws, concepts, and their relations. It was to describe instead particulars in their concreteness. Croce's approach preceded the one expressed in Wilhelm Windelband's 1894 attack upon the argument that history was a science, and by likening history to art, the Italian philosopher's position resembled the ones proposed by Wilhelm Dilthey in 1883 and by Georg Simmel in 1892. Subsequently Croce was to realize that this early statement of the relations between art and history was ambiguous. From it one would be tempted to infer that, like history, art, based upon intuition of particular objects, should represent also what was true and real. In this respect, however, we have seen that Crocean aesthetics differed from the theory advanced by Baumgarten.

By 1892, Croce had not recognized that history, as dialectically distinct from art, required philosophic concept along with aesthetic intuition for its expression. His clarification of this point was to wait until the 1909 publication of the *Logica come scienza del concetto puro* (translated as *Logic as the Science of the Pure Concept* [1917]), wherein Croce would define further his concept of the philosophic concept. (The outlines for the 1909 *Logica,* which appeared as a second edition, were presented in a 1905 article called *"Lineamenti di una logica come scienza del concetto puro."* [17]) Croce's elucidation of the nature of the concept occurred along with his distinction between purely intuitional awareness and intuition-as-representation that formed the subject of historical judgment. I am, however, reserving discussion of his later specification of intuition-as-representation, which required its organic synthesis with pure concept in judgment, for chapter 4, which treats the Crocean concrete-universal.

When Croce's essay of 1893 was published subsequently in the *Primi saggi,* the author acknowledged that he remained satisfied with his early demonstration of intuition as cognition. Moreover, his distinction between art and history on the one hand and the sciences on the other had answered this question: Is history a science? Unfortunately, neither scholastic logic nor the Herbartianism of Antonio Labriola, Croce's former professor at the University of Rome, had stimulated him to distinguish further between philosophic and scientific concepts. With regard to the conceptual difficulties that as yet he had not thought through, Croce assumed a provisional notion that involved a Platonic separation between a world of Concepts (eternal, ideal, and unchanging) and one of varying representations.

Prelude to the 1902 Estetica

Croce's next philosophical statements on intuition, art, history, and the empirical sciences occurred in a 1900 publication entitled *Tesi fondamentali di un'estetica come scienza dell'espressione e linguistica generale*[18] (Fundamental propositions of an aesthetic as science of expression and general linguistic), which was started in 1898. By *"scienza"* Croce meant *"Wissenschaft,"* or a body of systematically organized knowledge. The Italian word *"scienza"* did not possess the technical, inductive, deductive, and empirical connotations and denotations that "science" expressed in the English language. The *Tesi fondamentali* responded specifically to Giosué Carducci's attack upon De Sanctis's principles of literary criticism;[19] and generally to theoretical difficulties arising from the position that Croce had assumed in *"La storia ridotta sotto il concetto generale dell'arte."* Croce described thus his own state of mind prior to the writing of the 1900 work:

> when I set to work, and began to collect my scattered thoughts, I found that I knew little or nothing. The gaps in my knowledge multiplied as I looked; the things on which I believed myself to have a firm hold became indistinct and confused; and for nearly five months I read nothing, I walked about for hours together, I lay for half-days and whole days on the sofa, searching incessantly within myself, and jotting down notes and ideas, each a criticism of the last.[20]

These early writings were in some respects still the result of immature thought. Croce himself was to describe them as arid and abstruse. He retained his conception of intuition as cognitive and emotive. As such it provided the subject matter for art and history. Croce also reaffirmed Vico's thesis that language and poetry were substantially the same. However, Croce had not yet clearly distinguished between the disciplines of art and history. In other words, he had not differentiated between intuition as the subject of historical judgment and intuition as art. Nevertheless his critique of the use of a priori principles in literary criticism, his analysis of aesthetic genres, and his presentation of the four fundamental activities of the human spirit—intuitional, logical, economic, and ethical—were to be elaborated in mature doctrine. The *Tesi fondamentali* also reflected Croce's definitive condemnation of positivism and historical materialism, along with his identification of art with expression and language. Perhaps, however, its greatest significance lay in deepening Croce's understanding of problems which he then attempted to resolve in the writing of his 1902 *Estetica*.

The 1902 Estetica

In 1902, Croce offered his readers the *Estetica come scienza dell'espressione e linguistica generale* (*Aesthetic as Science of Expression and General Linguistic* [2d ed. rev., 1922]). His first major work on aesthetics (and unfortunately the only one read by some American philosophers) developed out of ideas contained in the *Primi saggi* and the *Tesi fondamentali*. The fundamental thesis that Croce had proposed in the *Primi saggi* remained the same: intuitional cognitions amounted to unique impressions and expressions of particular feelings. They formed the "objects" of art as well as history and were to be sharply differentiated from the universals and general laws that pertained to the empirical and abstract sciences. Since, however, intuition expressed "the as not yet differentiated unity of the perception of the real and of the simple image of the possible,"[21] how were art and history to be distinguished from each other? Croce did write that only with a conceptual understanding of what was "external and internal, of what has happened and what is desired, of object and subject . . . does it [consciousness] distinguish historical from non-historical intuition, the *real* from the *unreal,* real imagination from pure imagination."[22] Nevertheless, according to his own testimony, he still had not clearly demarcated history and philosophy from art as pure intuition. Indeed, when discussing whether history represented a third theoretical form of consciousness (besides intuition and concept), he merely repeated the title of his 1893 essay: *"La storia si riduce perciò sotto il concetto generale dell'arte."*[23] In Croce's own words, at that time he had not realized that "the possible" was dialectically distinct from "the real." Nor would he do so until he had clarified his own concept of the concept. For according to the 1902 *Estetica*, intuitions could become concepts and concepts pass into intuitions until it was sometimes impossible to distinguish between reality and fantasy. In such cases we "must either renounce for the time being at least the knowledge of what really happened (and this we often do), or we must fall back upon conjecture, verisimilitude, probability."[24] At this time Croce probably still accepted without question Vico's identification of primitive history with poetry.

A hint of the solution to what would emerge as a clear problem for Croce lay in his affirmation that history, unlike the empirical and abstract sciences, *did not arbitrarily construct* the concepts of the real and the unreal, but *made use of them.*[25] Croce would later explain the distinct natures of intuition and concept in terms of the differences between the various synthetic a priori acts of mind—aesthetic and logical. Although in 1902 he did recognize that with the advent of concepts, history became distinguished from art, the implications of his position— that is, that representation of a past event became a philosophical judgment when particular intuition and universal concept were synthesized in thought—were not as yet clear. Eventually both history and philosophy were to be fundamentally differentiated from art, as well as from the empirical and abstract sciences by means of the notion that philosophy was history, or to put it more precisely in Croce's terms, that philosophy was the methodological moment of history. This determination was one that Croce derived from his discussions with Gentile on Hegel. It became adapted to his philosophy of spirit and was worked out in the second edition of the *Logica*.

Intuition as Form

Still another development would be made in Croce's 1902 conception of ordinary intuition. The *Estetica* postulated that whatever spirit did not manifest represented a limit and a sine qua non for cognition. Intuition became distinguished as form from the "flux or wave of sensation, or from psychic matter; and . . . this taking possession, is expression."[26]

Subsequently Croce would maintain that, without intuition, one did not differentiate form from content. He came to ascribe this aspect of his 1902 conception of intuition to a residue of early Kantianism and naturalism in his *Tesi fondamentali*.[27] Croce's distinction between intuition as form and primitive sensation as content had also occurred in Vico's criticism of Plato for confining poetry "within the baser part of the soul, the animal spirits," for "poetry precedes intellect, but follows sense."[28]

Despite Croce's correction, it is apparent that intuitional expression continued to play the same role in his philosophy as Kant's "sensuous manifold," which yielded the material necessary for every conscious experience. Unlike Kant's sensuous manifold, however, the Crocean intuitions were immediately expressed, without being subsumed under the forms of space and time, and without the application of concepts.

Degrees of Complexity

I have described the Crocean intuition of 1902 as the form of cognition required for art and history. Let me now indicate how ordinary intuition was to be distinguished from intuition-as-art. The latter was marked by the complexity of its expression in comparison with the simplicity of mundane representation. Croce put it this way:

> The intuition of the simplest popular love-song, which says the same thing, or very nearly, as any declaration of love that issues at every moment from the lips of thousands of ordinary men, may be intensively perfect in its pure simplicity, although it be extensively so much more limited than the complex intuition of a love-song by Leopardi.[29]

A difference between intuition-as-art and ordinary aesthetic expression then was quantitative and impossible to determine a priori. Croce maintained thus that ordinary intuitions were less complex than the complicated and difficult expressions of art. By way of illustration, imagine the simplicity of an ordinary garden when compared with Hieronymus Bosch's *Garden of Earthly Delights*. We may contemplate both gardens without further thoughts about their reality or even their beauty (which would amount to transforming pure intuition into judgment). Clearly, however, the expression of Bosch's *Garden* would be the more complex image (Croce used the adjective *"estensiva"*) since it represented a garden perhaps more complicated and symbolically suggestive than any fashioned by nature itself. To summarize: the complexity of art did not bring with it a *qualitative* demarcation from non-art. For even a relatively simple intuition might be as perfect *sui generis* as the artist's complex imagery.

The Concept of Organic Unity

Degrees of complexity thus helped a critic to recognize the differences between ordinary intuition and art. We must, however, add organic unity as well to Croce's list of defining qualities:

> Another corollary of the conception of expression as activity is the *indivisibility* of the work of art. Every expression is a single expression. Activity is a fusion of the impressions in an organic whole. A desire to express this has always prompted the affirmation that the work of art should have *unity,* or what amounts to the same thing, *unity in variety.* Expression is a synthesis of the various, or multiple, in the one.[30]

In the Crocean view every genuine work of art was thus a synthesis or an interconnection of "qualia" (Croce himself did not use this term), which formed a unified whole. The relations among the qualia were felt as necessary and not fortuitous connections. If, in a complex feeling of this sort, any element should alter, the aesthetic constellation itself would change but could remain coherent. As an illustration, consider that with a somewhat altered last act, *Othello* would appear as a different play, but possibly a coherent one; or imagine *Hamlet* in its usual version and as it might appear without Ophelia, or *King Henry IV* lacking Falstaff; or visualize the *Mona Lisa* with her smile replaced by another, non-archaic one. However, as we have seen, organic unity also marked the difference between ordinary intuition and simple sensations or feelings merely juxtapositioned to one another. So it would seem that the definitive characteristic of art lay entirely in the quantitative complexity of its expression.

What of Non-Art?

Insofar as art did require the organic synthesis of images, some unsuccessful intuitions were marked by disunity or incoherence among their representations. Non-art displayed disconnected series of single intuitions. For the *immaginazione* (fancy), unlike the *fantasia* (mind's creative imagination), mixed and combined single elements in a loose and arbitrary fashion—much as the grains in a heap of sand are mingled with one another.

What amounted to non-art, furthermore, might not be intuition at all, but another type of expression—for instance conceptual, or practical in the sense of didactic. One could not determine a priori whether an expression might be intuition, art, or indeed another altogether different form of spirit. A critic was to reproduce as well as possible, within the limitations of historical circumstance, the original representation. He next was to categorize it as art or non-art. If the latter, the critic then could determine whether the expression was ordinary intuition, concept, or a form of practical and not theoretical activity.

Perhaps today when assonance along with discord and even disintegration are applauded in aesthetic creations, Croce's use of the concept of organic unity for determining the presence of art appears overly simplistic. Thus a work of art such as Picasso's *Guernica*, for instance, expresses a deliberate incongruity and sharp juxtaposition of images, which would apparently violate at least the "coherence of nature." Here, however, obvious incoherence serves poetic expression and thereby becomes, aesthetically, an essential ingredient in the artist's intuition. In other cases an artifact may be perfectly "coherent," but in a rather mechanical and unaesthetic sense. As illustrations, consider Salvador Dalí's geometrically precise *Last Supper,* or some of T. S. Eliot's verses in *The Waste Land.*

Moreover, although quantitative complexity characterizes some art, it does not describe other such creations. The aesthetic quality of Dante's poetry,[31] for example, in part lies in the rich complexity of its imagery; however, the opposite would be true for a Japanese *haiku*. Yet one would be reluctant to exclude the latter from the realm of art on the grounds of simplicity alone. In short, neither the criterion of quantitative complexity nor that of organic unity would appear to serve as a universal one for distinguishing art from non-art. Indeed Croce himself soon felt compelled to further characterize art. What were the developments (*svolgimenti*) in Croce's 1902 concept of intuition? And what prompted their occurrence?

Art as Lyrical Feeling

Like his earlier writings, the 1902 *Estetica,* instead of "emptying his head" of all that Croce knew, suggested further projects. Croce's initial description of art in terms of complexity and organic unity had satisfied neither himself nor the critics, and the determination of lyricality among its defining characteristics came about in order to distinguish better ordinary intuition from art.

The use of "the lyrical" as an evaluative criterion thus developed generally out of Croce's work with poetry and literature as genres. It was Croce's task as editor of *La critica* to review Italian literature published during the preceding fifty years; Gentile was to treat the history of Italian philosophy. Croce himself confirmed that "the conversion of my first concept of intuition into the further concept of pure or lyrical intuition was not due to an inference from the first, which taken by itself satisfied me and remained inert, but to suggestions arising from the actual practice of literary criticism, as I wrote my notes on modern Italian literature and reflected directly upon works of art and tried to harmonize my former thoughts with the new thoughts that thus arose."[32]

Specifically, Croce arrived at the concept of lyricality as a reply to Giulio Augusto Levi's critique of the first editions of the *Estetica* (1902) and *Logica* (1905), although as early as 1904 Croce had used the terms *"motivi lirici"* and *"personalitá,"* which according to Gian Orsini anticipated what was to come.[33] In his *Studi estetici* (1907), Levi, an Italian aesthetician, had acknowledged two forms of intuition—immediate and mediate.[34] The first consisted of contemplation, a state of mind, or a feeling, and it occurred in the creation of poetry or art. With mediate intuition, however, a person reflected upon his immediate awareness and composed history as well as scientific thought. In *La critica*, Croce evaluated Levi's critique of the Crocean intuition: an emphasis upon the lyrical quality of expression marked a *development* and *not* a contradiction of his concept of art as pure intuition. At this time, Croce wanted merely to understand better the character of aesthetic feeling. He did not consider a closer rapport between the fundamentally diverse intuition and concept.[35] When Croce reflected upon the development of his thought since the 1902 *Estetica*, he saw progress in the gradual elimination of a dualism between intuition as form and the feelings that were its source as content, a growing emphasis upon the spiritual unity of human expression, and a deepening of the meaning attached to the conception of intuition.[36]

In his Heidelberg lectures of 1908, Croce elaborated upon this further qualification of art as lyrical feeling. His opening passages contrasted five aesthetic concepts: empirical, "practical," intellectual or rational, agnostic, and mystical.[37] Croce considered whether these conceptions had occurred in all historical periods and, moreover, in the aesthetics of every thinker. Did they also exhaust the attitudes we can assume toward art?

Croce determined that the order of the concepts as given above was a historical and dialectical one, wherein each concept, preserving the truth and rectifying the errors in the preceding, incurred problems to itself as well. Subsequently he would acknowledge the influence of Hegel upon this aspect of his thought. His view that the history of aesthetics expressed a dialectical order which culminated in Croce's own theory of intuition had occurred also in the 1902 *Estetica*. It would be replaced by a problematic approach, which meant that philosophic inquiry was to be conducted via problem solving. This treatment was to assume the literary form of the *saggio* or monograph. One of Croce's earliest expressions of his new treatment of philosophy was to be seen in his 1907 book on Hegel, *Ciò che è vivo e ciò che è morto della filosofia di Hegel.*

What did each of the five aesthetics propose? Every empirical conception of art presupposed a set of aesthetic "facts." An *"estetica praticistica"* held that we could categorize these facts as expressing a definite form of human spirit. Rational aesthetics, for its part, asserted that the category of art belonged not to the practical but to the theoretical sphere of human activity. And the truth of agnostic or "negative" aesthetics lay in supposing that art belonged not to a category of logic but to another, undetermined one. For Croce, however, even agnostic aesthetics expressed a contradiction. It assumed a cognitive form, superior to philosophic knowledge, yet defined and explicated by the latter.[38] An agnostic attitude toward art did recognize the errors of the previous concepts—empirical, "practical," and intellectual—but was unable to provide a solution for them. The so-called mystical aesthetics encountered further difficulties when it claimed that art as a spiritual form was ineffable, or worse when it proposed that art amounted to play.

Croce urged us to reject a mystical approach to aesthetics and to recognize that art was indeed pure intuition. He argued that in comparison with other kinds of cognition, intuition was the most simple and fundamental. It included neither the concepts of historical narrative nor the classification of an empirical science. Intuitional cognition expressed images only and yielded concrete rather than abstract knowledge. Art as pure intuition, Croce concluded, was also essentially lyrical: *"l'intuizione pura è essenzialmente liricità."*[39] Croce gave us phenomenological descriptions of lyrical quality. It lay in "the life, the movement, the emotion, the fire, the feeling of the artist; only this gives us the supreme criterion for distinguishing works of true art from false, the successful from the mistaken. When emotion and feeling are present, much is forgiven; when these are lacking, nothing can compensate for them."[40]

How did Croce view the addition of lyricality to the defining qualities of his 1902 conception of art? "Lyricality," he claimed, was simply a synonym for intuition, although it also represented a deepening of his understanding of aesthetic expression as feeling or emotion. Indeed Croce's embellishment did not appear to be either an entirely new concept of art or a contradiction of his earlier one. But still another qualification of intuition, cosmic totality, was to follow lyricality. Its reconciliation with Croce's 1902 concept of art as the expression of particular images would prove far more difficult for aestheticians than had his concept of the lyrical.

Art as the Expression of Cosmic Totality

Croce's 1918 essay entitled *"Il carattere di totalità dell'espressione artistica"* ("The Totality of Artistic Expression" [1966]) further determined the Crocean concept of art by describing another important characteristic—aesthetic universality. Although Croce did not elaborate his concept of the aesthetic universal before 1918, there were at least earlier suggestions of what was to come. The 1913 *Breviario di estetica* (*Guide to Aesthetics* [1965]), for instance, proposed that a kind of "aesthetic universality" was intrinsic to the intuitional process, inasmuch as art consisted of an aesthetic a priori synthesis between feeling and image within intuition. Artistic representation expressed, moreover, the *universe* regarded *sub specie intuitionis*.[41] There were, still earlier, somewhat ambiguous passages that acknowledged the eternality of art. These writings, however, may refer to its perennial occurrence as the result of the transcendental activity of human consciousness, rather than to art as an expression of the cosmos. Or they may reflect a remnant of Croce's initial Platonic Herbartianism. Nevertheless, in the preface to the fifth and subsequent editions of his *Estetica* (1922), Croce claimed that the germs of his definitions of art as lyrical and cosmic were present in the 1902 edition of that work. Perhaps he saw a suggestion of his concept of cosmic totality in the attribute of *"estensiva,"* which art, but not ordinary intuition, possessed, although we have seen that this adjective implied mere *quantitative complexity*. It could thus include works of art that the category of cosmic totality would exclude, and vice versa. On the one hand, for example, Jackson Pollack's *No. 8, 1949* represents a quite complicated aesthetic image. Still, it is not clear that its expression is universal in Croce's sense. On the other hand, Henri Matisse's sketches of nudes or Piet Mondrian's *Composition in Red, Blue, and Yellow* portray comparatively simple images. Nevertheless these works may well express what Croce meant by character of totality. However, the more important question here is not whether Croce's concept of cosmic totality was present as such in his 1902 work, but whether his elaboration of the aesthetic universal was consistent with his concept of art as the expression of a particular and unique object.

Upon reading these allusions to a concept that only subsequently was to be elaborated, one might wonder why the aesthetic universal had not been more fully developed before the publication of the 1918 essay. Indeed Croce himself acknowledged that other doctrines, developed prior to his own, had recognized the aesthetic universal, albeit unfortunately by linking it to philosophy and religion. He wrote thus that in general "the fact that the representation of art . . . encompasses everything and reflects the cosmos, has been noted many times."[42] And he credited specifically Wilhelm von Humboldt's 1797–98 essay *"Hermann und Dorothea"* as having expounded the universal or cosmic character in artistic representation best of all its proponents.[43]

An answer to this puzzle may lie in the fact that before 1910, Croce had been struggling against the dominance of the neopositivistic school in aesthetics. He was intent then upon stressing the particularity of intuition as art, when distinguished from the historical concrete-universality of philosophy and the "absolute" universality of the abstract sciences. By 1918, however, Croce became engaged in a polemic against excesses quite different from the positivistic ones. A reaction against scientism had led to irrationalism in Italian literature; the leader of this neoromantic movement was Gabriele D'Annunzio. Croce turned his attention accordingly toward the negative influences, as he saw them, that stemmed from the romantic reduction of art to merely individualistic or egoistic expression. The Italian philosopher-critic described his own perspective thus: "Now, however, after a century and a half of Romanticism, may it not perhaps be well that Aesthetics should throw light rather upon the cosmic or integral character of artistic truth, the purification from particular inclinations, immediate forms of feeling and passion, which this calls for?" Indeed for Croce, modern literature of the last century and a half had amounted to a series of confessions. Characteristic of its style was "an abundance of personal, particular, practical, and autobiographical outpourings."[44]

Along with Croce's debates with fashionable literati, his continuous work as a critic of writers whom he was to describe as *"poetici cosmici"*— Ariosto, Corneille, Shakespeare, Dante, and Goethe, for instance— probably helped to inspire the elaboration of cosmic totality. Some critics (Joel Spingarn, for example) had complained about the omission of the aesthetic universal from Croce's commentaries. He probably felt that lyricality did not suffice to differentiate the works of great writers from less distinguished ones.[45] If so, this explanation would illustrate once again the dialectical movement between theory and practice that pervasively characterized the evolution of Crocean philosophy.

What did Croce wish to convey by the phrase "aesthetic universal"? He referred to it as both *"carattere cosmico"* (cosmic character) and *"carattere di totalità"* (character of totality). Inasmuch as he used these phrases interchangeably, it seems reasonable to assume that they possessed the same meaning. Croce did not define the aesthetic universal as a special lyrical motif that, with respect to the unique richness and intensity of its ethos, became distinguished merely quantitatively among other themes. The character of art lay in the lyricality *and* totality of its representation. Nor by "embraces the whole, and reflects in itself the cosmos" did Croce mean that great literature, for instance, need amount to a treatise on metaphysics, although passages from Lucretius's *De rerum natura* and Dante's trilogy did qualify as aesthetically cosmic. Croce did not wish to suggest that pictorial art must portray the galaxies, even though the emotive subject matter of such a work as Van Gogh's *Starry Night* might well reflect cosmic universality according to Croce's sense of the term. Nor was "character of totality" to imply that art became transformed somehow into all four fundamental expressions of consciousness—intuitional as well as conceptual, economic, and ethical. To quote Croce on this point: "For Art is pure intuition or pure expression, not Schellingian intellectual intuition, not Hegelian logicism, not the judgment of historical reflection, but intuition wholly pure of concept and judgment. . . . And its character of totality can be understood without our having ever needed to issue forth from the limits of pure intuition, or to undertake readjustments or, still worse, eclectic additions."[46] The autonomy of intuitional feeling was retained thus in relation to the other three forms of consciousness, when they became *transformed* into cosmic expression. And the unique quality of aesthetic expression as compared with ordinary intuition was elaborated. This point, I believe, was made again very clearly in Croce's 1933 Oxford lectures entitled "The Defence of Poetry":

> If, then, poetry is intuition and expression, the fusion of sound and imagery, what is the material which takes on the form of sound and imagery? It is the whole man: the man who thinks and wills, and loves, and hates; who is strong and weak, sublime and pathetic, good and wicked; man in the exultation and agony of living; and together with the man, integral with him, it is all nature in its perpetual labour of evolution. But the thoughts and actions and emotions of life, when sublimated to the subject-matter of poetry, are no longer the thought that judges, the action effectually carried out, the good and evil, or the joy and pain actually done or suffered. They are now simply passions and feelings immediately assuaged and calmed, and transfigured in imagery. That is the magic of poetry.[47]

The essence of great art lay not in its apparent subject matter but in the depth and breadth of the artist's emotional expression, which allowed us imaginatively to move beyond characteristics peculiar to our own culture and age. The emotive ethos of cosmic art, for Croce, exceeded thereby the limitations of geographic origin and historical period. It occurred, for instance, in the works of such otherwise "opposite" poets as Ariosto and Shakespeare. Cosmic quality lay in their expression of "the constant rhythm and also . . . the variety of life that is born, expands, is extinguished and reborn, in order to grow and be extinguished anew."[48] The recognition of aesthetic totality required empathy and the acknowledgment that this particular expression resonated in the heart of every person.

Cosmic Totality: A Negative Statement?

The Crocean concept of art evolved thus from "intuition as complex feeling" to "lyrical expression" and to "cosmic universality." Croce himself wrote that these embellishments represented developments and not contradictions of the 1902 *Estetica*. With regard to his elaboration of the aesthetic universal, however, some commentators have not been as sanguine as Croce has appeared to be. How are *we* to consider these developments from the point of view of both his aesthetics and the relations between the two theoretical forms of consciousness—intuitional and logical? Had Croce thereby denied a fundamental difference between aesthetic and logical activity? Do such alterations, if considered from within the framework of his doctrine, represent an attempt to bridge the gap of kind and nature between intuition and concept? [49] Indeed a doctrine of the logical nature of poetry—that is, of art as philosophy or religion—once prevailed in German idealism. Recently it has reappeared in the aesthetics of such actual-idealists (the followers of Gentile) as Ugo Spirito. Nevertheless, Croce himself denied such an interpretation, and a careful reading of his works will not support it. [50] For Croce, intuitions could never possess logical universality. Genuine art reflected instead a kind of "emotive universality," which perennially allowed it to be recognized and felt as such. Croce's aesthetic universal thus evolved out of his experiences of the *alogical* qualities of art, to which the categories of judgment did not apply.

A second question is whether intuition itself can represent both the particular and the universal. [51] Some commentators have argued that early in Croce's career he had expounded a "positive" view that intuitional feeling is particular. [52] Afterwards Croce confusedly asserted that within aesthetic experience, the individual and the cosmic indistinguishably unite. These critics have interpreted the attribution of the "universal and individual" to the *object* of expression as a "negative statement," contradicting Croce's earlier theories.

How can we answer these objections? Would Croce's aesthetics remain viable, for instance, if universality were predicated of the creative act, whereas the aesthetic image remained particular? Or was the artist-critic unable to separate *totalità* from art only when he judged it by reflective thought?[53] Must aesthetic harmony, at best metaphorically describable as "cosmic," remain a particular feeling?[54] Unfortunately these questions may imply that we can consider either the intuitional process or its images in abstraction from one another. In the Crocean aesthetics, however, such an abstractive process was not possible. Indeed, when only one of these factors becomes emphasized, Croce's views tend to be misinterpreted.[55] We would encounter further problems by phrasing the particular and the universal qualities of art in terms of relations between object and subject.[56] Traditionally, epistemological as well as metaphysical realists have used dualistic language when expounding their theories. Gnoseological idealists, however, tried to avoid such terminology in their descriptions of cognition. They believed that during the act of knowing, an organic unity prevailed between consciousness and its "contents": neither became conceivable as separated from the other. In this respect Croce's doctrine did not differ from what his idealist predecessors had maintained. His essays, written prior to the *Estetica,* did discuss intuition and the "object" of art. His major works on aesthetics, however, generally avoided "subject-object" phrases. For Croce such thinking became an unfortunate by-product of various theories of nature that philosophers had expounded during the Renaissance. Logically speaking, an object was nothing other than spirit: *res* as *res* did not exist. Accordingly, it was to be conceived *within* consciousness—as a necessary moment, and as the most elementary form of the practical.[57] "Objects" were the desires, feelings, and emotions of mind's "economic activity." They did not occur in the theoretic realm, and we should not attempt to find them there.

As we have already seen, early in his career Croce had not expressly predicated *"totalità"* of artistic creation. That aspect of intuition, which was not separable from its activity, was an image. The latter was particular and individual, in contrast with *pure concepts,* which displayed *logical* universality. In his *Breviario di estetica* of 1913, however, Croce proposed that a kind of "aesthetic universality" was intrinsic to the intuitional *process.* But did he also maintain that its representation remained particular? The content of this essay did not warrant an affirmative answer. For here art was, in some sense, the universe regarded *sub specie intuitionis*.[58] Do we recognize this cosmic attribute solely by ratiocination? Croce held, on the contrary, that within intuition the cosmos was not *logically* explicit:

> It is useless to retort that the individuality of the image does not occur without reference to the universal, since the image *is* the universal individualized. But here . . . we deny that in intuition as such, the universal, is *logically* explicit and thought.[59]

For Croce, aesthetic creation was particular, yet also concretely universal. Indeed, the feeling that formed the essence of art became individual and concrete only when it acquired *"totalità,"* which happened whenever a particular representation expressed the feelings of "everyman." Croce judged Ariosto's *Orlando* and Dante's *Inferno,* for instance, as masterpieces, because such literature manifested *specific* images that fused into an organic unity and expressed the emotions—the hopes, fears, and desires of humankind: "In every intonation of the poet, in every creature of his imagination, there lies human destiny—all the hopes, the illusions, the pains and joys, the greatness and the miseries, the entire drama of reality, which endures and thrives perpetually on itself, in suffering and rejoicing."[60]

What was the source of cosmic character? Form conferred universality upon the passionate content of art and consisted of the rhythm, meter, color, and tones that one cannot conceive apart from any object. In his 1918 essay on the aesthetic universal, Croce asserted: "To give, then, artistic form to sentimental content is to impress upon it simultaneously the imprint of totality, the breath of the cosmos; and in this sense, universality and artistic form are not two, but one."[61] We should intuit thus the harmony of feelings, the work of art, as a fusion of the cosmic with the particular; and recognize a kind of totality, within both act and image, not as simply one of these determinants.

Commentators have argued that Croce's assertion that aesthetic representation was both particular and universal expressed a contradiction that invalidated Croce's concept of intuition. Within the context of his own philosophy, however, the use of a logical criterion such as contradiction to evaluate aesthetic, alogical expression resulted in what Croce

described as a "category mistake." For each of the activities of consciousness—intuitional, conceptual, economic, and ethical—expressed concepts that were appropriate to it: to confuse or misapply
them amounted to categorial error. An understanding of this point,
however, depends upon a comprehension of all the elements of judgment and their various types. Accordingly, I plan to reserve further explanation of such criticism until my final chapter. In my opinion, it was
Croce's categorial theory that provided an original contribution to
philosophic thought.

Another way of looking at the various determinations of the Crocean
concept of art is from the perspective of his view of philosophy as provisional. We would see, then, that his doctrinal embellishments remained consistent with the philosopher's fundamental task: to appropriate what was living in the history of thought, to discard what was
false, and to transcend former "truths." Croce acknowledged that propositions have appeared to contradict one another.[62] Simply to affirm totality of a set of conflicting judgments, however, would not resolve the
problem caused by contradiction. Croce's solution was that some of
these statements were ultimately resolved in a wider verity, one that
both included and somehow *transmuted* earlier inconsistencies. This
passage taken from his *Guide to Aesthetics* illustrates his thought:

> The subsequent life of the spirit, by renewing and multiplying prob-
> lems, makes preceding solutions not so much false as inadequate, some
> of which fall into the group of those truths that are understood im-
> plicitly, while others need to be reconsidered and integrated.
>
> A system of thought is like a house which, right after being built and
> decorated, requires for its upkeep an effort more or less vigorous but
> assiduous (subject as it is to the corroding action of the elements). Now,
> at a certain moment it is no longer worth repairing and propping but
> must be demolished and started from scratch. Yet there is, to be exact,
> this major difference between the two, namely, in the work of thought,
> the perpetually new house is perpetually maintained by the old one—
> which . . . persists in the new.[63]

If we grant Croce's concept of the dialectical movement of thought,
along with his theory of error as privation or partial truth, then his rec-

ognition of the "cosmic" in art formed a "wider truth" that would also include the earlier one—that is, that art was both particular and universal in its immediate expression. Far from being a "negative statement"—to be understood metaphorically—Croce's theory of intuition, if considered thus, continued to specify the unique character of human aesthetic experiences.

Perhaps Croce himself would have recommended that when we investigate the feelings that compose art, we should not make too much of *words*. We should inquire instead: Is their expression merely particular, like that of ordinary feeling, or do they include and yet surpass the particular with a cosmic quality clearly designating them as art? If our answer is a resounding "yes," then our next query would read: In what respects did the Crocean aesthetic universal differ from the logical? Let us now turn our attention to those differences and treat Croce's concept of the concept.

4

The Sphere of Logic

I have proposed that Croce's philosophy underwent a lifelong process of self-criticism and internal development. For this reason we must explore the pervasive theme of thesis and transcendence in order to understand its nuances. The transformation of Croce's ideas can then be linked by the rationale appropriate to them. Croce's concept of the concept demonstrated the very point that the whole Crocean structure, not merely the aesthetic, rests upon this interpretation.

The Concept of the Pure Concept

The Crocean concept of the concept, like the Italian philosopher's theory of intuition, evolved during at least the early years of his long and distinguished life.[1] Indeed, some commentators have maintained that throughout his entire career Croce held two or even three fundamentally irreconcilable views of its nature: an early Herbartianism presented in the 1893 essay on relations between art and history and maintained up to the working out of the 1902 *Estetica;* a post-Hegelian position affirmed from his 1907 *Ciò che è vivo e ciò che è morto della filosofia di Hegel* (translated as *What Is Living and What Is Dead of the Philosophy of Hegel* [1915]) to his 1952 *Indagini su Hegel e schiarimenti filosofici* (Inquiries on Hegel and philosophical clarifications); and finally in the last-named work, a rejection of his post-Hegelian conception of the category coupled with a return to the Hegelian concrete-universal. Critics have also attempted to show that a late emphasis on the economic concept of *vitalità* (vitality or vital force) suggested that Croce was tending toward a reduction of the various categories of the human spirit—aesthetic, philosophic, economic, and ethical—to the economic one.

My own opinion is that early in his career, while under the influence of J. F. Herbart's doctrine, Croce did adhere to a Platonic view of the eternal, unchanging nature of the philosophic and scientific concept. During the first decade of the twentieth century, however, he developed a Kantian conception of the *origin* of the pure concept as issuing from the logical synthetic a priori activity of consciousness.[2] But he disagreed with Kant on other major points, such as what terms were to be included in the realm of concepts, as well as on the relations that held between them. Although universal in its expression, the Crocean concept exhibited the concreteness and historicity of the Hegelian concrete-universal. Yet as a gnoseological (nonmetaphysical) and directive category of historical narrative, the pure concept also differed from the Hegelian universal in fundamental respects, a difference I shall discuss later in this chapter.[3] Croce's position thus could not be reduced to either a Kantian or a Hegelian one; until his death he continued to maintain a unique concept of the concept especially suited to his own philosophy of the human spirit.[4]

Historical Background

During the years 1886–92, immediately following Croce's departure from the University of Rome, the Italian scholar became aware of a need for categories of interpretation and directive concepts in historical narrative. At that time he was absorbed with research on the history of the Kingdom of Naples and the relations between Italy and Spain. But the historian soon wearied of filling his mind with "lifeless and disconnected facts at the expense of much toil and with no constructive result."[5] While attempting to solve specific difficulties of hermeneutical research, Croce turned to the general topics of history and knowledge. With their explication in mind, he studied Italian and German books on the philosophy and method of history, including for the first time Giambattista Vico's *New Science*.[6] Out of the various perplexities that had beset Croce while pursuing his historical investigations came his first philosophical work, *"La storia ridotto sotto il concetto generale dell'arte,"* which temporarily organized his logical and methodological ideas. In this essay of 1893 on the relations between history and art, Croce did not differentiate between the conceptual natures of philosophic and scientific objects. For him both disciplines dealt with universals and their relations. He provisionally adopted a kind of Platonic theory of their eternal and unchanging nature in contrast to the varying objects of sense perception.

Immediately after the publication of *"La storia,"* there followed another period (1893–94) of intense historical investigation of the relations between Spain and Italy. Croce's inquiries were interrupted by the writing of a short book on the *method* of literary criticism[7] to "expand and clarify a discussion with a professor of philology."[8] To his surprise this work proved controversial; but even before discussion about it ceased, he returned to studies of Italo-Spanish relations. His historical research was eventually broken off, this time by Antonio Labriola's invitation to read the first of his essays on Karl Marx's conception of materialism. Croce's subsequent work with Marx's philosophy would result in the adoption of a third category of historical interpretation, the economic, besides the aesthetic and philosophical ones.[9] In his autobiography, Croce described the significance of this period in his life:

> And the study of economics, a conception which from the point of view of Marxism is identical with that of reality as a whole, or philosophy, brought me back to philosophical problems, especially to those of ethics and logic, but also to the general conception of the spirit and its various modes of operation. These thoughts, like my economic studies, were all directed towards history as their ultimate ends; for I long intended to return to my historical researches armed with my new weapons of economics and historical materialism.[10]

In a manner thus analogous to the development of the Crocean intuition out of the requirements of literary criticism, the evolution of the concept issued from his work as a practicing historian. Croce's view of the relations between the theoretical and practical forms of consciousness once again was mirrored in the rhythm of his own life between theory and praxis. Years later when he reflected upon that early decade of erudition and inquiry without benefit of guiding principles and directive concepts, he wondered that

> an ardent reader of De Sanctis like myself, who ought to have known by heart every word of his doctrine that erudition without philosophy is neither criticism nor history but mere formless matter (and no doubt I did know every word of it, but not by heart, for I repeated the words without grasping their full sense), could spend so long in the pursuit of erudition with philosophy, in mere antiquarianism. . . . Yet, if I had not done this, I could never have thoroughly and firmly understood De Sanctis' central thought, the transcending of mere erudition.[11]

The development of Croce's mature concept of the concept, however, would have to wait until after the publication of the 1902 *Estetica*. There he did acknowledge an empirical sense of rhetorical categories that he excluded from the *philosophy* of art. By this recognition, however, he meant that "*verbal variants* of the aesthetic concept" were "no longer in the service of art and aesthetic, but of *science* and *logic*."[12] Thus Croce still had not worked out clearly the differences between the pure concepts of philosophy and the empirical and abstract pseudoconcepts of the inductive and deductive sciences. The reason for this continued obscurity probably lay in his concentration on the nature of intuition along with its relations to art, history, and the sciences, to the neglect of his concept of philosophy and history. Subsequently Croce developed his theory of the gnoseological differences between the two fundamentally diverse kinds of science—philosophical on the one hand and empirical and abstract on the other. At the same time he also clarified what he had called the theoretical and practical forms of human experience—cognition and volition.

What was to become of Croce's mature concept of the pure concept was introduced in his *Lineamenti di una logica come scienza del concetto puro*

(1905; Outlines of a logic as science of the pure concept) and *"Ciò che è vivo e ciò che è morto della filosofia di Hegel"* (1906; What is living and what is dead of the philosophy of Hegel) and then developed in his 1907 book on Hegel under the same title as the 1906 essay, and in his 1909 *Logica come scienza del concetto puro* (translated as *Logic as the Science of the Pure Concept* [1917]). The *Logica* gave us one of the Italian philosopher's earliest formulations of the logical (as distinguished from the aesthetic, economic, and ethical) synthetic a priori activity of consciousness that created the Crocean universal. He ascribed this important tenet of his philosophy to Immanuel Kant's influence on his thought. According to Croce's view, however, it was not a mechanical but a creative activity that produced a new, original, and even unexpected object. [13]

In the aesthetic a priori synthesis, image and feeling formed an organic unity. What were the elements necessary to philosophical expression? The logical a priori issued from an interconnection between universal concept and particular intuition. Here the latter became transformed into what Croce called a "representation." Such transmutation amounted to a change from an atemporal expression to one that implied the historical existence of intuition. In this way the unieversality of the concept became concrete. The logical synthetic a priori expression of consciousness that formed the pure concept thus operated, not in a void, but with intuition. By the publication of his *Ciò che è vivo e ciò che è morto della filosofia di Hegel,* there were no Crocean abstract concepts in the Platonic sense of Forms or in the Cartesian one of clear and distinct ideas. I will withhold further discussion of this point, however, until the section on what Croce called individual or historical judgments, since a full consideration of the Crocean a priori synthesis should include treatment of his theory of judgment. Let us now focus our attention instead upon the nature of the pure concept and how Croce differentiated his view from the Hegelian concrete-universal.

Concepts and Their Relations: Croce and Hegel

In his examination of what was living and what dead in Hegel's doctrine, Croce discussed the German philosopher's concrete-universal in its relationship to intuition, empirical concept (general representation), and abstract term:

> Philosophic thought is for Hegel: 1) concept; 2) universal; 3) concrete. It is *concept,* and that means it is not sentiment or ecstasy or transcendental intuition, or any other similar psychical state, alogical and indemonstrable. . . . The philosophic concept is *universal,* and not merely general: it should not be confused with general representations, which, for example, the house, the horse, the color blue, are put to barbaric use, as Hegel says, when they are ordinarily called concepts. . . . The philosophic universal, in short, is concrete, which is to say that it does not consist of arbitrary abstractions: it is not isolated from reality, but comprehends reality in all its richness and fullness: the philosophic universals [*astrazioni*] are necessary, and thereby correspond to the real, and do not mutilate or falsify it. . . .
>
>   . . . the true concept, the philosophic concept, appears logical, universal and concrete.[14]

In this passage Croce affirmed that Hegelian concepts were concrete and universal. As logical expressions of mind, they were distinguishable from mere feelings (*sentimenti*) and pseudoconceptual empirical and abstract terms. Philosophic concrete-universals corresponded to what was real and did not mutilate, falsify, or exist detached from reality. Yet by virtue of the universality of its expression, every pure concept transcended the particular concrete representation that was its source. In short, the Hegelian concrete-universal was neither a purely transcendental or abstract idea, nor an entirely historical and arbitrary empirical concept.

At this point Croce apparently believed that his own conception of the concept agreed with the Hegelian one in regard to logicality, concreteness, and universality. Subsequently, however, he was to describe his reaction to the Hegelian dialectic as follows: "Such a wearisome 'ballet of bloodless categories,' finding a final rest in one supreme ultimate category is precisely the 'panlogism' or pure rationalism which weakened Hegel's vitality and effectiveness and against which I rebelled."[15] What was, for instance, the origin of the concept of morality, if not an "engraftment on the trunk of our special impulses and individual passions, hot with the blood of life, grimy with the grime of life, of which it is not a negation but a function and an expression." [16]

Croce, moreover, did not concur with Hegel's view of the dialectical relations that held among these logical forms. According to the Crocean view, seemingly "opposed" or "contradictory" terms such as "beauty" and "ugliness" were interrelated, not as two concepts, but instead as a concept and its privation or negation. By way of illustration: "the ugly" was included in "the beautiful" as the expression of what might have been more beautiful, and "the evil" was present similarly in "the good" as representing a degree of the latter. Every privative term (for instance, "ugliness") necessitated a positive one ("beauty") for its occurrence:

> It is indubitable that opposite concepts neither are nor can be reduced to distincts. . . . Beauty, truth, utility, moral good are distinct concepts; but it is easy to see that ugliness, falsehood, uselessness, evil cannot be added to or inserted among them. Nor is this all: upon closer inspection we perceive that the second series cannot be added to or mingled with the first, because each of the contrary terms is already inherent in its contrary, or accompanies it, as shadow accompanies light. Beauty is such, because it denies ugliness; good, because it denies evil, and so on. The opposite is not positive, but negative, and as such is accompanied by the positive. [17]

Contrary, then, to Hegel's application of the so-called theory of the opposites to relations among conceptual expressions, Croce held that none of the pure concepts was joined dialectically to another contrary one so that their synthesis formed a third concept. He put it this way: no concept could be deduced or developed from another in an orderly progression by demonstrating the logical self-contradictions of the first concept. [18] To summarize: a Crocean concept was related to its "contrary" solely in the modality of positive term and privation. As a consequence, what Hegel saw as opposite concepts—for example, the ugly, the false, and the evil—were not so at all for Croce, but represented privations of concrete-universals. Indeed the Italian philosopher held that the relation between a concept and its negation differed markedly from the interconnections that occurred among concepts themselves:

The true does not stand in the same relation to the false as it does to the good; the beautiful does not stand in the same relation to the ugly as it does to philosophic truth.[19]

The Theory of the Distincts and Degrees

How were the pure concepts linked to one another? Or, to use Croce's terminology, what was the theory of distincts that played such an important role in formulating the Crocean concept of the concept? The Italian philosopher himself acknowledged: "As is widely known and understood, the *leitmotif* of my mental labours has been a sturdy defence of the concept of 'distinction.'"[20] "Distinct," however, did not mean separate, inasmuch as each concept was connected with every other, such that taken all together, they formed a unity. The philosopher was to comprehend and explicate the differences among the concepts with the unitary principle elaborated in Croce's theory of degrees.

Conceptual interrelations manifested themselves in necessary and hierarchical arrangements. These interconnections, called "degrees" or "grades" (*gradi*) by Croce, were held together by implication. The logical relation of "imply" that linked the *concepts* to one another also reflected the phenomenological relations that occurred among *activities of consciousness*.[21] There were thus no subdivisions of the concept considered exclusively as a logical form, since the concepts represented the various activities of consciousness and were not deduced from possible types of judgment only. By "phenomenological" I mean that the grades of the concepts were not existentially, temporally, or spatially distinct. Logical forms were distinguishable instead in terms of function and origin: "Each form, then, has its own function, and its own place in the order of succession, and each is in turn the form of a precedent material and the material of a succeeding form. It follows that none is, in an absolute sense, first or last."[22] To illustrate: just as logical expression required its representation via intuition, the concept of philosophy implied that of art. The concept of the economic implied those of philosophy and art; analogously, economic will depended for its occurrence upon conception as well as intuition. There were no empty philosophical terms, and will was never altogether irrational or blind. Phenomenologically, praxis followed theory, and the concept of man's volitional activity implied that of theoretical expression. This view represented the Crocean rendition of the rationalist dictum that the real was rational. In the passage that follows Croce summarized his theory of degrees or the hierarchical ordering among concepts:

> What does the theory of degrees mean? Which are its terms, and what is their relation? Moreover, how does this theory differ with respect to the terms and to the relations of the theory of the opposites? In the theory of the degrees, every concept—let it be, the concept *a,*—is simultaneously distinct from and united to the concept, which is superior to it, *b;* according to which . . . if *a* occurs without *b, b* cannot occur without *a.* Taking up again, for example, the relation between the concepts . . . art and philosophy (or between poetry and prose, or between language and logic or between intuition and thought, *et seq.*), we see how what is an insoluble enigma and puzzle for empirical and classificatory logic, is resolved naturally in speculative logic, by means of the doctrine of the degrees. It is not possible to suppose art and philosophy to be distinct and coordinate species of a "kind" [*genere*], to which both are subordinate and which might be, for instance, the cognitive form and in a way such that the presence of the first excludes the other, as is the case for coordinate members. . . . art does not include philosophy, but philosophy directly includes art. And in fact, no philosophy ever exists save in words, images, metaphors, forms of speech, symbols, which are its artistic side, a side so real and indispensable that, were it wanting, philosophy itself would be wanting.[23]

The reader might assume that by "superior" Croce meant that philosophy was in some sense qualitatively better than art and analogously that the theoretical sphere was inferior to the practical one.[24] I have found no justification for such an interpretation of Croce's logic, however. By this perhaps unfortunate adjective, "superior," he wished to indicate instead that the concepts were linked asymmetrically. We have already seen that this hierarchical order of conceptual dependency was also exhibited by the interconnections among various conscious activities.

Croce argued further that Hegel's incorrect view of the relations between concrete-universals led to two erroneous conclusions. The first
was that philosophic errors or privative terms became valued as partial
concepts. In this case what Hegel would have treated as two opposing
concepts—being and nothing, beauty and ugliness, truth and falsity,
for instance—Croce affirmed as concept and its privation. The second
result was that true judgments were taken to be philosophic errors and
"nothing other than imperfect forms of philosophy."[25] As a consequence, Hegel had failed to recognize the genuinely autonomous nature of art, since he held that every philosophical form of consciousness
amounted to a merely incomplete and self-contradictory conception of
the absolute. The structure of Crocean aesthetic expression, however,
unlike the Hegelian, did not exhibit an inherent contradiction. In this
respect art *qua* art was a complete representation of the human spirit.
Hegel's view, on the contrary, had claimed that "artistic activity is distinct from philosophy only by virtue of its imperfections, only because
it gathers the absolute in sensible and immediate form, whereas philosophy fathers it in the pure element of thought. This means logically
. . . that art . . . is reduced substantially . . . to philosophic error, or
an illusory philosophy."[26] Here I would like to mention in passing that
until after the writing of the 1908 Heidelberg lectures there was a dis-
crepancy between Croce's theoretical statements and what he assumed
in historical narrative. In historical narrative, as we saw in chapter 3,
Croce did indeed interpret the history of the concept of art, for instance, as exhibiting degrees of truth that culminated in his own concept of art as intuition. Subsequently, however, he adopted his problematic approach to philosophy, never to return to what he described as
a residue of Hegelianism.

The 1952 Book on Hegel

Some commentators have argued that until the writing of his 1952
Indagini su Hegel e schiarimenti filosofici, the Italian philosopher had ad-
hered to the conception of the pure concept described in the preceding
section. In this work, however, published during the year of his death,

the Crocean concept of the pure concept supposedly became transformed into something akin to the Hegelian concrete-universal. In fact
Croce did assert that a kind of "opposition" (*opposizione*) was generated
from the distinct nature of the categories with the result that "each
strives to persist beyond its own realm [*ufficio*]." Such opposition
amounted to a kind of *"bellum omnium contra omnes."* [27]

Other critics have proposed that Croce's Hegelianism appeared in
early literary criticism. For instance, an essay on Shakespeare's sentiment, included in his *Ariosto, Shakespeare e Corneille* (1920), emphasized the expression of positive and "negative" (not to be understood as
"privative") qualities—good and evil, joy and pain, liberty and necessity, reality and appearance. Here these terms were presented as unresolved coincidences of opposites, such that the negative terms of evil,
pain, necessity, and appearance did not represent merely a degree of the
positive ones but were in a sense "equally strong in Shakespeare's feeling." They were, moreover, "entwined in conflict, without reconciliation in a superior harmony." [28]

How then are we to interpret these passages in the light of Croce's
repeated assertions that his own philosophy had appropriated what was
vital in Hegelian doctrine and discarded what was irrelevant, specifically the theory of the opposites? Is this an illustration of an unresolved
inconsistency between the author's theory and practice or does it provide evidence of a latent Hegelianism? It is my opinion that neither was
the case. In the critical essay on Shakespearean sentiment cited above,
Croce also wrote that there were "facts," which *the poet* could *neither
explain nor resolve philosophically.* These were *intuitions* that occurred entirely on the level of feeling, whereas concepts along with their unique
relations could never be substituted for feeling states. The poet was to
represent sentiments, which subsequently the philosopher could mas-
ter and alter by conceptualizing them. In this manner feelings became
transformed by rational thoughts into concepts. No doctrine could be
extracted thus from Shakespeare's "prephilosophy," since the expression
of opposing feelings differed fundamentally from an understanding of
concepts and their relations to one another in terms of privation and the
theory of distincts and degrees.

Even if we grant that Croce could give a reasonable response to our questions by appealing to fundamental differences between the characteristics of feelings and concepts, how are we to understand his 1952 statement that "opposition arises in all the categories"? I would propose that here Croce was referring to "the contradiction that is inherent in the real which is becoming."[29] Since, in the Crocean view, each category implied all the others, their implicatory relations need include the pure concept of becoming, or the passage from one to another.

Moreover, in the same essay, wherein Croce wrote of the "opposition that is generated from the *distinct* nature of each concept," he also warned that if for emphasis a category should become treated by itself, the reader should never forget that each referred to all the others, since "their distinction is also unity, unity of the spirit."[30] Even more significantly, he never proposed that the categories synthesized to form a "higher" concept that included and yet transcended the "lower" ones. No concept represented thus a mere "fragment of reality" that must supersede itself to form a higher synthesis and a more complete logical expression. Instead the Crocean view described the movement of human conscious activity as circular. When it expressed itself intuitionally and then conceptually, it did not pass to a higher degree of reality or truth. Indeed reality and truth themselves were concepts and as such were not present in aesthetic expression. Perhaps Croce's philosophy becomes easier to understand if we keep in mind that the Crocean concrete-universals were not metaphysical entities. Rather they represented activities of consciousness, and the links between them reflected the interconnections among the expressions of knowledge and will. As long as Croce maintained that the various activities of the theoretical sphere remained distinct although unified by human consciousness, the relations among the concepts could not be dialectical in Hegel's sense of that word.

All of these considerations suggest that Croce did not return to a Hegelian theory of dialectical change. If he had accepted the German philosopher's dialectic, then logical consistency would have forced him to alter his particular approach to philosophy via its problems and to return to the kind of historical narrative presented in his first *Estetica* and in the 1908 Heidelberg lectures—one that Croce subsequently discarded and attributed to an early Hegelian influence upon his phi-

losophy. The autonomy of art and the uniquely Crocean distinction between philosophy and history, with the former as the methodological
moment of historiography, would have been disavowed. Finally, his
categorial theory of error, which depended upon the theory of distincts
and degrees, could no longer be maintained.[31] For similar reasons recent efforts to interpret all the Crocean categories as expressions of human economic spirit are bound to fail. Indeed some critics have argued
that Croce's late emphasis upon the economic concept of vitality demonstrated that he himself was moving in that direction. If a kind of
economic reductionism had been Croce's own intent, then fundamental
revisions of his aesthetic, his definition of philosophy and history, and
the concept of the ethical vis-à-vis that of the economic also would have
been required. And in this way the uniqueness along with the enduring
value of the Crocean philosophy would perish. I for one cannot imagine
Croce ever arriving at such a conclusion.

We have discussed the Crocean concept in its relations both to intuition and to other concepts. Our treatment, nevertheless, remains incomplete, since a concept that did not express a judgment of a particular object was as unreal in the Crocean system as an intention that was
not an action. When working on his 1909 *Filosofia della pratica,* Croce
himself discovered that a dualism was present in the first edition (1905)
of his *Logica* (*"Lineamenti di una logica"*) between the concept and sin-
gular judgment, that is, between philosophy and history. He then recalled his discussions with Giovanni Gentile on the Hegelian identification of philosophy and history; determining to adapt that position to
his own philosophy of the human spirit, Croce carried out his plan in
the 1909 edition of the *Logica.* Let us now examine Croce's theory of
judgment and see exactly how it expressed the organic a priori synthesis
of intuition with concept.

Propositions and Pure Judgments of Definition

Croce defined propositions as simple expressions of imagination whose
cognitive form was predominately intuitional. Strictly speaking, they
occurred solely in the sphere of the aesthetic, and like intuitions, these

aesthetic expressions did not refer to reality or unreality, nor to truth or error. Only when a transition from proposition to definition was completed did such concepts and logical values occur.

Pure judgments of definition, sometimes called logical definitions and judgments, consisted entirely of concrete-universals and were explicitly or implicitly answers to questions or solutions to problems. Croce characterized these purely logical expressions in the passage that follows:

> For every definition is the answer to a question, the solution of a problem. Did we not ask questions and set problems, there would be no occasion for giving any definition. . . . Not only does the answer presuppose the question; but every answer implies a certain question. The answer must be in harmony with the question; otherwise, it would not be an answer, but the avoiding of an answer. . . . This means that the nature of the question colours the answer and that a definition taken in its concreteness is determined by the problem which gives it rise. The definition varies with the problem.[32]

The same verbal formula could amount to proposition in one context and a logical judgment in another, depending on which cognitive form—intuitional or logical—dominated.

> Taken by themselves, any verbal expressions which we adduce or can adduce as proofs are indeterminate and therefore of many meanings. "Love is life" can be the saying of a poet who notes an impression with which his soul is agitated and marks it with fervour and solemnity; or it can be, equally, the logical affirmation of someone philosophizing on the essence of life.[33]

Although aesthetic proposition and definition were distinguishable, they were not altogether separable from each other, since definition was organically synthesized with proposition. In Croce's words: logical judgment (thought) was a "crystalization" of aesthetic proposition (language); the relationship between such expressions was analogous to the interconnection between intuition and concept.[34] According to Croce, aesthetic proposition was phenomenologically prior to logical judgment, inasmuch as judgment included proposition in its expression, whereas the reverse did not hold.

We have seen that a judgment of definition (for example, intuition is a theoretic form of spirit) explicitly expressed concepts only. But because for Croce any real distinction between subject and predicate required that a universal concept be predicated of a *particular* subject (for example, Michelangelo's *Pietà* is a work of art), no such differentiation between the terms of pure definition can properly be made. Croce described this type of judgment thus as "tautologous" and as analytic a priori, since the ultra- and omnirepresentative expression of each concrete-universal must include that of every other. If in logical judgment the extensions of subject and predicate completely overlapped, then what did the copula "is" express? Here is Croce's response to this question:

> As to the "is," since the two distinct terms which should be copulated are wanting, it is not a copula; nor has it even the value of a predicate, as in the case in which it is asserted of an individual fact that it is, that is to say, that it really happened and is *existing*. The "is," in the case of definition, expresses nothing except simply the act of thought which thinks; if it were not, it would not be thought; if it were not thought, it would not be. The concept gives the essence of things, and in the concept *essence involves existence*.[35]

The existence of a concept in definition became represented by the act of thought that expressed it; in this sense conceptual existence was implied by the essences of both subject and predicate.

Individual or Historical Judgment

Definition, however, did not exhaust Croce's inventory of logical statements. He described those judgments whose constituents did not consist exclusively of concepts as "individual" and "historical." In a statement of this type—such as "The legal abolition of slavery widened the degree of liberty that had existed in the United States of America"—the subject had been a complex intuition; but when organically synthesized with a conceptual predicate "liberty," it lost its purely aesthetic character and became what Croce called a "representation."

How did pure intuition differ from representation? Chapter 3 showed that intuition was unique, particular, but explicitly devoid of concepts such as truth, reality, or logical universality. When intuition occurred in judgment, however, it implied its own historical existence. Croce put it this way:

> every individual judgment implies the existence of what is spoken of, or of the fact given in the representation, even when this fact consists of an act of imagination, so that this fact may be recognized as such and as such existentialized.[36]

In individual judgments, unlike pure definitions, "existence" did not mean merely the act of thought that thinks, for their subjects were concrete objects or events. Thus "existence" did not coincide with essence. In what sense then was "historicity" implied by the subject of such a judgment? Croce maintained that in individual judgment "existence" or "existent" was to be understood as a predicate, that is, as adding to the meaning of the subject. A representation supposedly implied its historical reality by virtue of its organic unity with a concept in judgment. And because each concept was linked to every other, the "existence" of the subject was necessarily implicit in any judgment that included concepts.

> It therefore only remains to conclude that in the judgment all possible predicates are given in one act alone; that is, that the subject is predicated as existence, and for this very reason determined in a particular way; determined in a particular way, and for this reason as existence.[37]

Croce's claims notwithstanding, in the above passage "existence" turned out to be purely conceptual and his argument was a circular one. In short, the existential status of representation was implied by its synthesis with a pure concept that in turn entailed its own existence. The reader is left once again with an act of thought that thinks, and any difference between "existence" as implied by the subject of a Crocean definition (for instance, "Thought is a theoretic form of spirit") and by the representation of historical judgment ("The *Mona Lisa* is a work of art") has been verbal only. Let us take another look at the sort of "existence" supposedly implied by representation. Did historicity originate from intuition rather than concept? Did Croce, for instance, hold that space and time were qualities inherent in aesthetic experience?

Space and Time

As early as the 1902 *Estetica*, Croce had argued against Kant's theory of the a priori forms of sensibility and proposed instead that spatial and temporal attributes were not inherent in every type of cognition. Croce thus eliminated these coordinates from the sphere of the aesthetic when he maintained that intuition per se bore no reference to them.[38] In the Crocean philosophy the synthetic a priori of intuition provided the foundation for art but not for geometry and mathematics. When Croce developed his view, he may have reflected upon the difficulties in holding that purely imaginary objects as they served as subjects of judgments were located spatially and temporally.

If space and time did not qualify aesthetic experience, were they then pure concepts? In his *Logica*, Croce maintained that their "ideal nature" (*"idealità del tempo e dello spazio"*) represented one of the great philosophical discoveries of Kant. However, he also wrote that the mathematical concepts "space" and "time" (or as he put it "the entire conception of things as occupying various portions of space and following one another in a *discontinuous* manner, separated from one another in *time*"—were derived from quantitative pseudojudgments. Croce thus excluded these conceptual fictions from the realm of the pure concepts and asserted that they had been developed for practical ends from an ingenuous conception of reality suggested by perception. Space and time when understood in this sense "should be called not ideality (because ideality is true reality), but rather *unreality* or *abstract reality,* or, as we prefer to call it, *abstractness.*"[39]

It still remains to ask what Croce might have meant by the *ideal* nature of space and time. "Becoming" and "development" were ultra- and omnirepresentative pure concepts that expressed the essentially unified and continuous (not contiguous) character of reality. Nevertheless we have already seen that any appeal to the concrete-universals for the purpose of determining the existential differences between the subjects of historical judgment and definition was bound to fail. All of these considerations lead me to conclude that the presence of space and time, understood either in a mathematical or even in an ideal sense, could not account for the historicity of representation. Instead, its existential status must be explained via the creative nature of the logical synthetic a priori act that originated it. To illustrate: in Croce's judgment that "Homer's *Iliad* expressed the tragic feeling of life, which was fundamental to every true poetry (art)," the subject (*Iliad*) represented a historical object in its organic synthesis with a Crocean universal (poetry). The concrete aspect of the concept required the poetic feeling that was its source. Yet intuition in itself was ahistorical. Historicity, then, originated as a *novel* element out of the organic unity and logical a priori synthesis that linked intuition with concept. It could not be attributed simply to either element but was given a posteriori in a phenomenological inspection of the synthesizing activities of the human spirit.

Now that we have reviewed the differences between definition and individual judgment, let us examine their relations to one another. Croce held that the interconnections between these types of judgment were implicatory and symmetrical. The passage that follows describes how on the one hand an individual judgment implied a definitory one.

> The passage from intuitions to the concept, and thereby to the expressions of the concept or definition, and from this to the individual judgment, has been traced and demonstrated in its logical necessity; such that, the two distinct forms are entirely united, the first being condition and foundation of the second with a concreteness that seems perfect. The judgment of definition is not individual judgment, but the individual judgment implies a prior judgment of definition. Whoever thinks the concept of man, does not mean that the man Peter exists; but in order to affirm that the man Peter exists, it is necessary to have affirmed first that man exists, or to have first thought that concept.[40]

On the other hand, because every pure concept was historical as well as universal, each definition presupposed individual judgments whereby its constituent concepts were expressed. These links between pure and historical judgments formed the foundation for the interconnections between philosophy and history. There were no vacuous concepts; nor was narrative of the past blind or irrational. Written history thus was not to consist of chronicles of parliamentary records. On the contrary, it concretely illustrated a general theme based upon directive concrete-universals such as art, truth, and liberty. I heard a similar view stated by the historian Joel Hurstfield in a talk on the neglect of "liberty" as a guiding concept in the writings of twentieth-century historians. Indeed, according to Hurstfield, present-day history often lacks directive categories and becomes, for this reason, mere detailed record. To summarize: Croce concluded that any separation of definitory from historical judgment was abstract and hermeneutic.[41] Strictly speaking, these forms of judgment could not be disunited in the sense that each presupposed the other in its expression.

From his view of the reciprocal relations between pure definition and individual judgment, Croce concluded that there was no fixed line of demarcation between analytic and synthetic, a priori and a posteriori. Definitions were analytic statements, inasmuch as they expressed concepts only. Yet every concept in turn represented a synthesis of particular subject with universal predicate, that is, a synthetic judgment. In the latter, historical representation was gained a posteriori (from concrete experience), whereas its concept was an a priori one. Moreover, the formation of a posteriori representation depended upon an aesthetic a priori synthesis of feeling and imagination, whereas concepts were formed via a logical a priori act of mind that synthesized particular with universal. Here is how Croce himself put it:

> If analysis apart from synthesis, the *a priori* apart from the *a posteriori,* be inconceivable, and if synthesis apart from analysis, the *a posteriori* apart from the *a priori,* be equally inconceivable, then the true act of thought will be a synthetic analysis, an analytic synthesis, an *a posteriori a priori,* or, if it be preferred, an *a priori synthesis.*[42]

Although narrative of the past depended upon the judgments formed from pure concepts, many if not most of the statements that comprised written history did not include these universals at all. They expressed instead a relation between representation and what Croce named a "pseudoconcept"—that is, an empirical or abstract term. Let us now consider these conceptual fictions that formed so much of historical narrative. How did they originate? And what characteristics distinguished them from the pure concepts?

The Empirical Pseudoconcepts and Pseudojudgments

Pseudoconcepts issued from the synthetic a priori practical activity of consciousness and strictly speaking did not provide us with knowledge. Constructions of will yielded neither aids nor hindrances to the discovery of truth since truth, as a theoretic concept, was established entirely by relations among representations and concrete-universals. Volition was not logically but "practically" rational, in the sense of coherent and successful adaptation of means to ends. Human practical activity thus used empirical and abstract terms as instruments to gain immediate goals. Some critics have argued that because of his early debates with the positivists, Croce endowed these objects manufactured by human will with an inferior status vis-à-vis the concrete-universals.[43] Indeed it is true that only gradually did Croce come to realize the service that the positivists had rendered with their critique of Hegelian metaphysics. Nevertheless I must disagree with such an interpretation. The Crocean sphere of the practical with its pseudoconcepts never held a lesser position in relation to the theoretic pure concepts. At times, as we have seen, Croce used the adjectives "superior" and "inferior" to express the phenomenological relations of *dependency* that held among the expressions of the human spirit. He did not, however, mean that the pseudoconcepts were of inferior value than the pure ones. Instead he meant to describe the asymmetrical relations that held between theoretical and practical activity.

Those pseudoconcepts, which Croce described alternatively as "empirical class names," were what contemporary logic usually referred to as "class terms." Unlike the ultra- and omnirepresentative pure concept, the denotation of the empirical concept was limited to merely some particulars. An empirical concept—"horse," for example—referred to instances of the genus "mammal" but was not immanent in every aspect of reality, as Croce would have put it. The classes denoted by these fictional concepts (empirical pseudoconcepts) could be exhausted by a single intuition or representation (for example, the class whose member was a mutation), and such classes invariably were completed by a finite number of objects.

One of the most important characteristics that empirical pseudoconcepts possessed, one that distinguished them from the pure concepts, was accordingly "exclusiveness"—a quality that contemporary logic also attributed to empirical terms. The class of all dogs, for example, excluded the class of all cats, along with the class of all trees. Both the extension and the intension of such classes were limited, although Croce allowed that they were not necessarily mutually exclusive. Thus the class of mammals included that of dogs. Since, as we have seen, the denotation and connotation of the pure concepts completely overlapped. Croce maintained that the connections among the classes named by pseudoconcepts bore no resemblance to the distinctions that held among the pure concepts.

Empirical pseudoconcepts were expressed via pseudojudgments that were akin to nominal definitions. They classified objects and were formulated for the sake of expediency. To illustrate: the critic catalogued works of art in terms of genres in order to communicate feelings and thoughts about them, and the historian divided the past, which was essentially a process, into periods that aided memory and organized events. Croce described pseudojudgments as commands in which no "determination as to value" (*"determinazione circa il valore"*) was involved.[44] Frequently they stated the means one used to achieve a sought-after goal. A physician classified disease thus in order to diagnose and treat it.

Empirical statements could also be called "judgments of classification." Croce advised us that ordering objects in terms of types did not yield knowledge. For this reason, empirical judgment was not to function as a logical one, although at times it attempted to do so. An example occurred in the erroneous view that there were "truths of perception"—for instance, in the case of a stick that appeared bent in water but straight when not so immersed. Croce's analysis was that the real "error" lay in the empirical concept "stick" according to which the appearance of the stick immersed in water did not answer to its "true concept." Strictly speaking for Croce, perception was apart from truth or falsehood since here we were dealing with empirical concepts. Croce also contended that this kind of error encouraged the positing of something (to use the words of John Locke) "I know not what" whose existence was apart from mind, or to quote Croce, the positing of *"the Thing in itself."*[45]

What were the relations between these empirical judgments and individual or historical ones? Whereas in historical judgments the pure concepts completely "penetrated" their subjects, in empirical judgments conceptual fictions were "mechanically" adapted to representations. They applied a posteriori class names to representations. Moreover, according to the Crocean philosophy, the subject of an empirical judgment did not follow directly from intuitional experience, *phenomenologically speaking.* It derived instead from a historical judgment. Croce claimed that in this way one revised classification in accordance with concrete experience.[46] The literary genres, for instance, were redefined or augmented relative to the new expressions of art that occurred in every historical period. What would have been impossible in the Crocean system was that any of the pure concepts such as art not occur at all.

Every empirical judgment presupposed an individual one, much as the latter related to pure definition. In *"Hamlet* is a tragedy," for example, the empirical predicate merely *suggested* other class terms— "noble birth," "character," "fate"—but *presupposed,* phenomenologically speaking, the pure concepts "art" and "the lyrical." In short, the useful and arbitrary classification of *Hamlet* as a tragedy required, for Croce, the judgment that *Hamlet* was a work of art. In every empirical statement, subject and predicate were linked thus to representation and pure concept as expressed in individual judgment. Similarly the "is" of empirical statements was related to the pure concept "existence," in the same phenomenological respect that "will" depended upon "thought."

In the case of the empirical concept, however, "existence" was implied moreover by the class that the concept signified: "This animal is a monkey" implies, not only the existence of the animal taken as subject of the judgment, but also of that class of animals, of which the character has been abstracted, and the complex of characteristics which, under the name of a monkey, fulfills the function of predicate. An animal that does not exist and a class of animals that does not exist are not reducible to subject and predicate and do not give rise to judgment of any sort.[47]

The Abstract Pseudoconcepts and Empirico-abstract Pseudojudgments

We have discussed empirical judgments in terms of their relations to individual ones. Let us now attend to abstract concepts and examine the kind of expression that could be formed from them. In our outline of the Crocean philosophy we saw that the concepts used in mathematics (number) and in geometry (figure) were abstract. Like the pure concepts, they were universal but were not really representative since they expressed no existential content. In the Crocean view, neither a straight line, nor a perfect triangle, nor any of the numerical series, for example, possessed historical reality. Croce described these notions as mere "fictions." For practical ends, we arbitrarily applied them to objects.

Abstract concepts as such were not referable to historical events. For because of their homogeneous nature, one could not predicate them of heterogeneous things. As an example, Croce noted the impossibility of adding up a cow, an oak, and a poem. Even the expression "*abstract individual judgments*" was itself a "contradiction in terms." For what was particular, that is, historical, could not be abstract; nor could the abstract ever be particular. How then were we to apply these "fictions" to historical objects? Insofar as the empirical judgment classified what was essentially unique, abstract concepts were predicable of representations. The reduction of the heterogeneous to the homogeneous was "effected . . . by the formation of classes. . . . Individual varieties, which escape all numerical application, are thus subdued, and we obtain . . . things belonging to the same class, as for example oaks, cows, men, ploughs, plays, pictures." In this way, we could form the empirico-abstract judgments: "'These cows number one hundred,' 'these oaks are three hundred in number,' 'there are four hundred houses in this village,' 'it contains two thousand inhabitants,' 'there are two ploughs in this field,' and so on. Or we can say elliptically: '100 cows,' '300 oaks,' '400 houses,' '2000 inhabitants,' '2 ploughs,' and so on, as is done in statistics and inventories." [48] Croce called the procedure proper to empirico-abstract judgments "measurement." Empirico-abstract judgments, like empirical ones, were neither true or false. They nevertheless were continually used and indispensable for practical and mnemonic purposes.

Despite the phenomenological parity among conceptual fictions and pure concepts, there was a great disparity between Croce's notion of knowledge and science, and what ordinary language assumed. Indeed neither hypotheses, nor mathematical formulae, nor ideas belonging to the physical sciences and theorems of geometry amounted to cognitive expressions. These hypotheses, judgments, and propositions were to be considered as distinct from the realm or grades of concepts. One of Croce's most important tasks, with which he was concerned throughout his career, was to differentiate pseudoconcepts from concrete-universals and thereby to rectify category mistakes. By carefully distinguishing between the theoretic and the practical spheres, and by relegating empirical and abstract terms along with the methods appropriate to their construction entirely to the practical, Croce the philosopher believed that he had prevented the intrusion of conceptual fictions into the foundations of the philosophical disciplines, such as aesthetics, philosophy, and history. A famous illustration of his endeavor, to be discussed in the concluding chapter of this work, lay in Croce's critique of the doctrine of the literary genres. With the completion of this treatment of the Crocean sphere of human logical expressions, we are ready to examine his theories of truth and error. For we may predicate "true" solely of judgment and not of any constituent taken by itself.

5

Truth and Error

Benedetto Croce's theories of truth and error followed from his concept of the concept. Indeed one might well argue that Croce's coherence theory of true judgment itself reflected what *he* believed to be still vital in European philosophic tradition, whereas what I have called his categorial theory of error represented one of his original contributions to speculative thought. In my opinion, however, to turn Croce's conception of truth upon himself, his coherence theory along with his view of objective judgment were no longer viable and should have been discarded, whereas I would retain his categorial theory in a somewhat modified form. Let us now consider Croce's conceptions of truth and objectivity and see what kinds of problems they involve.

The Coherence Theory

Croce applied his coherence theory to single judgments as well as to their interrelations. For him a judgment was true to the extent that its predicate expressed a synthesized subject. Conversely, when Croce wrote of "false" judgment, he was referring to the incoherence of its representation. Such errors did not occur as positive values. This type of mistake presupposed, on the contrary, some absence of conceptual expression.[1] One falsified by omission or ambiguity when one's thought was incomplete, because either an essential ingredient was lacking or its component elements were not thoroughly unified.

Moreover, each true judgment, by virtue of the logical linkage among concepts, implied and thus was consistent with every other. What, then, were we to think of apparently incompatible judgments? Croce himself acknowledged that they occurred:

> All this . . . is not prophecy . . . but a suggestion of what paths moral consciousness and the observation of the present may outline for those who in their guiding concepts and in their interpretation of the events of the nineteenth century agree with the narrative given of them in this history. Others, with a different mind, different concepts, a different quality of culture, and a different temperament, will choose other paths, and if they do so with a pure mind, in obedience to an inner command, they too will be preparing the future well.[2]

Croce would reply to our query that such "contradictory" truths became resolved within a "wider one." The wider truth both included and *transformed* the contradictory ones. He put it this way:

> truth itself perishes, particular and determined truth, because it is not rethinkable, save when included in the system of a vaster truth, and therefore at the same time transformed.[3]

How were we to know when this so-called greater truth had been achieved? Croce did not give us any special marks by which it might be recognized. We already have seen that he rejected the use of empirical or scientific methods in determining veracity. "Interior verification," consisting in a sort of "reliving" of a historical event, was to confirm merely particular truth; he never proposed that this measure would establish a "vaster" one. It was moreover unlikely that this criterion could verify, for example, the "vaster truth" of Croce's own doctrine that was supposed to encompass and surpass all the particular truths in the history of philosophy.[4] Indeed in this case, the principle of "coherence" again proved unreliable, for Croce allowed that at any time even a broader truth may become inconsistent with other judgments and still later have to be transcended.[5] And finally, as Maurice Mandelbaum asserted in *The Problem of Historical Knowledge* (1938), the determination of the correctness of various contradictory judgments itself presupposed a questionable point of view:

> The contradictions inherent in two conflicting standpoints cannot be adequately judged by any third person, since this person himself has a standpoint. Thus Croce's advice to read partisan history, but to make allowances for its partisanship, is unfeasible: we ourselves are partisans. And further, on his own grounds, Croce has no right to criticize the current practice of historical writing in Germany, so long as this writing answers to a true need. If it be held that Croce's need is a deeper and more effective one than that of a National Socialist idealogue, a point has been raised which only the Absolute, and not Mr. Croce, can answer. To say that a neutral party can determine the truth in this case is to beg the question, for on the Crocean assumptions there can be no neutral party.[6]

If for any particular truth there was a greater one destined to encompass and transform it, how trustworthy was the former? What validity and veracity could it possess? Yet when considered within the framework of Crocean aesthetics, surely such judgments as "Ariosto's *Orlando* is a literary masterpiece" were as reliable as the logical truth "Intuition is a theoretic form of spirit."

On the one hand, *logically speaking* these particular judgments should not have been called "true" at all, since each concept already implied every other in its expression. Croce wrote:

> To think any pure concept means to think it in its relations of unity and distinction with all the others. Thus, in reality, what is thought is never a concept, but *the* concept, the *system* of concepts.[7]

As expressed, then, every judgment already involved all its implicates and implicants. There was no real possibility that a true judgment could become *transcended* and *transformed* within the "system of a greater truth."

On the other hand, *historically speaking,* how could any judgment at a given time imply all those temporally prior and posterior to it? With the transformation of each judgment, the entire system had to be altered if it was to remain coherent. Unfortunately Croce did not provide us with a criterion that, within the confines of his philosophy, would help us to resolve such difficulties. In my opinion Croce's coherence criterion of truth reflected a residue of Hegelianism that persisted in his philosophy. It did not aid him in the problematic approach that he developed subsequent to the Heidelberg lectures. And although he referred to the coherence theory throughout his career, its use served only to detract from the valuable contributions provided by the categorial theory.

Croce claimed that every true judgment was also objective, since as a historian he understood the need for objective as well as subjective narrative. Let us put aside for the time being our problems with his coherence theory and now consider what Croce meant by "objectivity."

Crocean Objectivity: Historical Background

In an early essay, *"Della possibilità e dei limiti del giudizio estetico,"* published in *La critica letteraria* (1894), Croce asked whether aesthetic judgment was absolute or relative. Did there exist an objective criterion of taste? By "absolute" he meant an objective characteristic that was recognizable by anyone, just as true judgment or the moral value of an act was supposedly knowable. We formulated a relative and subjective judgment, however, in accordance with our own individuality. There was no obligation to discuss it, just as we need not justify tastes and pleasures of love. Croce concluded that if a judgment were about the *nature* of art, it should follow from the critic's concept of art. If we appraised the aesthetic *value* of an artifact, then "we should refer no longer to the concept, but to the ideal of art; and this ideal possesses a nature that is relative."[8]

Still under the influence of Kant's distinction between form and content, Croce considered also whether one determined the value of form and content subjectively. He defined "content" as "the interesting," whereas aesthetic form amounted to the colors, sounds, and other features that made up a work of art. Persons judged both aspects of art subjectively in terms of capacity and personality: "If we regard even only what happens to us in individual life, we can clearly recognize the relative value of the content and form of art." At that time Croce maintained that there was no objective criterion of taste. Nevertheless subjective appraisals were valuable. Persons of genius and refined sensitivity rendered better, more accurate judgments than what was offered by those of immoral feeling and no culture: "Whoever judges art is referred, for the content as well as form, to the taste of the best."[9]

In the 1902 *Estetica* one finds possibly Croce's earliest assertion that standards of taste, which he there carefully distinguished from the ratiocination of concepts, were absolute—"with the intuitive absoluteness of the imagination." He proposed that the activity of imagination required for aesthetic judgment was inherent in human nature, along with "logical concept and practical duty."[10] Moreover, if one were to deny the role of imagination, one would negate logical truth and morality since they too depended upon creative imagination. The background and taste of all humans differed. How could one explain the occurrence of similar judgments? Croce's response was that given like culture, education, emotional states of critics, and the same artifact, comparable aesthetic expressions invariably followed. But what about these conditions? If either the inner state of an artist-critic or the physical stimuli—for example, the canvas and colors of a painting—altered, as of course they did over time, then various opinions might be rendered by the viewer.[11] This fact did not perturb Croce, for although aesthetic expression could not be duplicated exactly, critics did surmount the difficulties of reproduction that lay in the varieties of physical and emotional conditions. If this were not the case, he argued, then communication, which depended upon memory and repetition of stimuli, would have been impossible. Likewise historians of art should attempt to restore relics and "traces," and other investigators should reproduce the past in order to represent it correctly. According to Croce neither the "arrest of interpretation" nor the problems of restoration formed an insurmountable barrier for historians, who continually were discovering new sources that helped to synthesize broken tradition.[12]

Croce's Mature Conception of Objectivity

These ideas express Croce's early views on objective judgment. What was his mature theory of objectivity? In the Crocean philosophy "objective" did not describe an expression repeated without alteration as, for example, the color of litmus paper when one applied acid to it. Nor did this adjective refer to an event that had been perceived alike by a community of observers. The contrary was the case: representations or subjects never reoccurred exactly as such. Nevertheless, in aesthetic criticism, for instance, the fecundity of the human imagination permitted the continual perception of a beautiful expression. Croce maintained indeed that given that the artist-critic possessed sufficient background, his cognitive awareness of the lyricality and cosmic universality present in an aesthetic image must follow. Similarly with regard to historical narrative, provided that the investigator possessed the proper documents, capacity, and interest to interpret them correctly, he would formulate a true judgment. The relations among the subjects of the same statements, whether in aesthetic criticism or written history, were akin to "family resemblances." Such representations were not identical, but their similarity sufficed for objectively true judgment.

Nor did "objective" mean an expression or event that one could evaluate by means of quantitative measurement. Pure concepts and their representations occurred solely in the theoretic sphere. They did not permit treatment via empirical and mathematical methods, or the pseudoconcepts belonging to practical activity. The natural, physical, and social sciences were founded upon "representative terms," which referred to groups of intuitions arbitrarily delimited for practical reasons.

Finally, "objective" did not describe a quality adhering to an object, independently of its cognition. According to Croce, all past history (every event that was not consciously expressed by someone) was "dead history": "these dead documents exist to the extent that they are manifestations of a new life, as the lifeless corpse is really itself also a process of vital creation, although it appears to be one of decomposition and something dead in respect of a particular form of life." [13]

What then did "objectivity" represent in the Crocean system? And what was its origin? Croce's *"Aesthetica in nuce"* (translated and published under the heading of "Aesthetic" in the 14th edition of the *Encyclopaedia Britannica*)[14] claimed that objectivity was provided by the concrete-universal or predicate, whereas subjectivity resulted from the representation in judgment. According to the Italian philosopher, on the one hand, whoever denied the absolute character of aesthetic judgment, for instance, also negated the autonomy and value of art, since without objective value aesthetic concepts would have amounted to descriptions of what was merely pleasing. On the other hand, whoever neglected its subjective aspect failed to recognize that the subject of a true judgment derived from the interests and needs of the critic. Croce concluded that one could not *separate,* although one could distinguish, the subjective from the objective qualities present in true judgment (just as these qualities could not be demarcated within the expression of the concrete-universal itself). Inasmuch as the critic or historian could not understand or interpret representation without concept, nor even concept without representation, subjectivity and objectivity never occurred in abstraction from each other.

Objectivity: Internal Criticism

How might we evaluate the Crocean conception of objectivity? Let us look at Croce's uses of "objective" first from the point of view of internal criticism. When considered from within the framework of his philosophy, has the presence of objectivity in judgment been sufficiently demonstrated? We have learned that Crocean objectivity depended upon the universal nature of the pure concepts. True judgment was objective, because its concept referred to every aspect of actual and possible reality. The expression of a concept, however, was via its representation, which as determined by the interests and needs of the historian was subjective. How, then, could the nature of the pure concept, which consisted entirely of its expression, account for objective judgment, since according to Croce whatever was not expressed did not occur?

Croce would reply that the subjectivity of representation became "transcended" with the conditions for true judgment. Its determinates included agreement among authorities, attested evidence and documents in written history, as well as the interests of the critic, historical exegesis, and taste with respect to aesthetic criticism.

Indeed, Croce held that all criticism—whether in the form of historical narrative or aesthetic critique—presupposed background knowledge, although that alone did not suffice for true judgment. The passage that follows dealt specifically with written history:

> philological history remains without truth as being that which, like chronicle, has not got truth within it, but derives it from the authority to which it appeals. It will be claimed for philology that it tests authorities and selects those most worthy of faith. But without dwelling upon the fact that chronicle also, and chronicle of the crudest, most ignorant and credulous sort, proceeded in a like manner by testing and selecting those authorities which seemed to it to be most worthy of faith, it is always a question of faith (that is to say, of the thought of others and of thought belonging to the past) and not of criticism (that is to say, of our own thought in the act), of verisimilitude and not of that certainty which is truth. Hence philological history can certainly be *correct,* but not *true* (*richtig* and not *wahr*). [15]

Thus even philological history that appealed to documents and authorities could be merely "correct" but not "true," since history written by witnesses ("correct history") was neither true nor false. In short, truth did not result necessarily from archival research, although it might well occur after an investigation of traces. Analogously, aesthetic criticism was not to consist merely of description or commentary, for then one simply dated the artifact and noted what it represented. Here too linguistic norms and historical allusions, along with the facts and ideals presupposed by a work, became explained. Such critique could be useful. It was not, however, genuine because it amounted to mere interpretation, commentary, or simply exegesis. In all of these instances the critic neglected the artist's spontaneous feeling, which evaluated his work according to personal taste. Although Croce held that none of these conceptions taken by itself was correct, nevertheless *all three*—art, taste, and historical exegesis—*were to be included within a wider notion of evaluation.*

In the final analysis, the interest of the historian or critic, the context, the evidence supplied by exegesis, and agreement among authorities became superseded in objective judgment. Indeed if historical data and probable inference only sufficed, then narrative or critique could consist entirely of empirical and abstract pseudojudgments. These somewhat arbitrary statements, as we have seen, originated from perception and compilation of data. But they formed what Croce himself called "chronicle" or "philological history" and not "true history," which issued instead from what Croce described as an *interior verification* of the *reality* of the historical object.[16] The historian was to pronounce the object of his investigations as *"Res tua agitur,"* meaning that he was to relive imaginatively the subject of his research.

History depended thus upon the reproduction of representation stimulated by evidence and judgment, which "qualifies the real according to one aspect of the concept and excludes another, or qualifies it indeed according to all its aspects, but distinguishes them, and therefore prevents the one from intruding upon the other."[17] By "qualifying the real" Croce meant that the task of critical reflection was to make explicit the concepts that directed historical interpretation. The philosopher investigated the activities of human spirit, which were intuitional, logical, economic, and ethical. Autocritical thought thereby established its categories for understanding objects. These guiding concepts included, for instance, in aesthetics, expression (lyrical and cosmic) and "the beautiful"; in logic, truth, judgment, and synthetic a priori; in economics, "the useful," the immediate goal; and in ethics, "the good," the relatively universal end. Representations were to be considered thus in terms of their aesthetic, philosophic, economic, moral, or even more generally, theoretic or practical properties:

> Thus, the human mind cannot think history as a whole, save by distinguishing it at the same time into the history of doing and the history of knowing, into the history of practical activity and the history of aesthetic production, of philosophic thought, and so on. In like manner, it cannot think any one of these distinctions, save by placing it in rela-

tion with the others, or with the whole, and thinking it in complete history.[18]

In an analogous fashion, the critic was to become the artist-creator as well as the judge of the work being evaluated. The fundamental problem present in critique was also one of determining the *reality* and the *quality* of the expression that represented a work of art. When addressing the critical process Croce wrote:

> The critic is not *artifex additus artifici,* but *philosophus additus artifici.* His work is not achieved until the aesthetic image becomes preserved and simultaneously transcended. The critic's task pertains to thought, which, as we have seen, overcomes and clarifies the creative imagination with new light. Thought transforming intuition into perception, qualifies the real, and thereby distinguishes reality from unreality.[19]

Clarification of intuition and transcendence of imagination, however, became possible only by linking representation with pure concept. Once again objectivity appeared to be redeemed by conceptual expression, which, as we saw at the outset of our critique, begged the question: Has Croce convincingly demonstrated that in judgment the subjective particularity of intuition-as-representation was concretely universalized, and not merely generalized as in empirical and abstract pseudojudgments? The core of history according to Croce consisted of the individual *sub specie universalis,* not of practical generalizations. Indeed in my opinion we have come full circle in our discussion without having conclusively resolved the problems inherent in the Crocean view of objective judgment. Let us therefore leave internal criticism and evaluate his conception from an external point of view by examining some of its presuppositions. Is it possible to avoid or even solve problems encountered in our internal critique by altering some of Croce's fundamental assumptions?

Objectivity: External Evaluation

If every true judgment is "objective," how are we to interpret that adjective? It has many uses in philosophy and in common parlance, of course. Some of these meanings, however, can be excluded here. Following Croce, I shall speak solely of the application of "objective" to judgment. (In doing so I shall, for example, avoid questions about types of qualities and in what sense mental events are "subjective" rather than "objective.") With respect to judgment, it is commonly claimed that a judgment is objective only if it be either true or false. While I would accept such a characterization of "objective,"[20] Croce would not, since in terms of Crocean theory an expression was objective only if it were a true judgment. Yet even here various problems existed. Let us consider how they arose within the framework of Croce's doctrine of the theoretic sphere.

We have seen that after the publication of the 1902 *Estetica* Croce discarded the Kantian postulate of the noumenon and thereafter maintained his phenomenology of the human spirit. Croce expressed his coherence theory of truth and objectivity thus within a philosophical position that he described as post-Berkelian "absolute" or "new" idealism. Although later in his career he preferred the label "absolute historicism,"[21] his epistemology did not fundamentally change. By "idealism" and "absolute historicism" Croce meant that the existence of an object depended upon its expression by consciousness. Indeed it is fair to say, I think, that Croce did deny the existence of anything that bore no relation to mind. In other words, he denied "absolute existence" or existence as a nonobject for rational consciousness. To restate his view in positive terms: whatever existed must have been conceived in relation to consciousness. Mind was foundational to reality in the sense that the synthetic a priori logical act was the source of the categories of historical interpretation. The world existed solely as a manifestation of human spirit, and nature could be understood only insofar as it bore the stamp of *lo spirito*. Croce's epistemology thus affirmed objects and qualities in their possible and actual relations to consciousness only and denied any object or quality that claimed ontological status independently of such relations.

In the Crocean philosophy the tenet that every objective true judgment expressed an immediate, logical state of mind followed from his epistemic idealism. His conception of judgment as an expression of consciousness led him to propose that history itself was "contemporary."

By this assertion he meant that the subject matter of judgment was created by the historian's present interests and reenacted in his imagination. Croce argued in this way:

> But if we look more closely, we perceive this history already formed, which is called or which we would like to call "non-contemporary" or "past" history, if it really is history, that is to say, if it means something and is not an empty echo, is also *contemporary,* and does not in any way differ from the other. As in the former case, the condition of its existence is that the deed of which the history is told must vibrate in the soul of the historian, or (to employ the expression of professed historians) that the documents are before the historian and that they are intelligible.[22]

Crocean history amounted, moreover, to autobiography, inasmuch as it issued entirely from the unique perspective of the historian's consciousness:

> . . . it is my solid conviction that every serious and clear history may be and ought to be "autobiography," that is, enter into the mind of the writer as his very own drama, such that he feels and says to himself about every event of it: *Res tua agitur.*[23]

If, as Croce claimed, history was contemporary and autobiographical, then it must consist of reconstruction of merely the inner states of a historian. But is this really the case in objective narrative? Or is there implied in the process of historical reconstruction a reality or event that is independent of and transcends our knowledge of it? By "independent" I mean that what is evaluated is not exclusively a product of conscious activity. In short, Croce's claim that narrative expressed solely conscious states patently contradicts the usual opinion of objective judgment, as well as that of historical inquiry. Ordinarily we do suppose a real difference between judgment and its "object"—whether the judgment be that an event has occurred, or that a document (to be understood in its widest sense as "evidence") is correct. Judgment according to Crocean philosophy was indeed followed by practical activity, which then stimulated theoretical expression. But these diverse activities—theoretical and practical—were expressions of consciousness, and thus the "epistemic circle" of purely conscious expressions remained unbroken. Here we did not have an alienation between subject and object, between consciousness and nature (considered as fundamentally other than spirit).

Analogously in aesthetic criticism, Crocean objective judgment was contemporary and autobiographical. But is this really the case? Does the critic in fact suppose that his judgments reflect simply his immediate awareness—albeit intuitional and logical? Or is critical response provoked by an "object" whose appearance is not determined solely by one's cognitive powers? Surely the very task of criticism presupposes that its "object" remains "independent" of judgment and in some important respect "the same" for the critic and his audience. Yet, as we have seen, according to Croce the work of art was never repeated. These contradictions between Croce's view and what we ordinarily suppose about the relationship between historical event or aesthetic object, on the one hand, and judgment, on the other, do not disprove Croce's conception of objectivity; they do, however, give us good reason to examine its presuppositions, since Croce's unsatisfactory theory of judgment may derive from the inadequacy of his assumptions.

Croce's Methodological Assumptions

We saw in chapter 2 that the Crocean method of philosophy consisted of a "psychological" speculative one. But by "psychological" Croce meant that philosophic inquiry was one of "introspection," to be understood in the sense of self-examination. The philosopher was to investigate the forms of expression, theoretical and practical, implicit in human consciousness. Croce described his method as "speculative" to distinguish it from any form of empiricism. Philosophic inquiry purported to make explicit pure concepts or categories that could not be discovered by empirical means. In this way philosophy became the "methodological moment," as Croce put it, of historiography. By this characterization Croce meant that the task of critical reflection was to make explicit the concepts that directed historical interpretation. The philosopher investigated the activities of human spirit, which were intuitional, logical, economic, and ethical. Autocritical thought thereby established its categories for understanding events. Philosophy became concrete, insofar as it interpreted and categorized the real within the historical context of each problem. Thus, the philosopher was not to determine or to resolve merely one issue, nor even to trace the history of ideas. Rather, as philosopher-historian, he was to treat problems arising out of some special concern. (In his later works, Croce came to define this interest as practical and moral.) In short, philosophy was a *process* of autocritical reflection, stimulated by contemporary and living questions. The literary form appropriate to philosophic inquiry was the monograph (*saggio*), which treated the problem and resolution that occupied the mind of the philosopher.

Although Croce himself held conceptions of philosophy and history that were derived from his epistemological idealism, his exhortation to know one's self has occurred throughout the history of ideas. We see it in the philosophies of Socrates, Hobbes, Spinoza, and others whom we would not ordinarily describe as "epistemological idealists." Furthermore, the results of the application of this imperative have varied significantly among these thinkers. Indeed, Croce's own self-discoveries suggest these queries: Did his claim that history amounted to autobiography commit the error of reductionism, by which I mean oversimplification? In other words, is there something inherent in historical judgment itself that renders Croce's claim impossible? Did it *neglect* an aspect of cognition that does not result from conscious activity of mind or will? My answer to all these questions is an unqualified yes.

Guiding Principles and Methodological Changes

In our evaluation of such questions what guiding principles and methodological changes should *we* propose? Instead of investigating the nature of merely mental and volitional expressions, we need to look at experience in general, at the way the world presents itself to us. I would not exclude (as Croce's speculative approach did) the use of a second method for gaining truth—for example, an empirical one. (The reader should recall that, for Croce, pseudojudgments were neither true nor false.)

What are some implications of these alterations of Crocean philosophy? By considering experience as it presents itself, without taking into account the influences of mind and will, we have allowed for the possibility that reality may transcend our consciousness of it. This starting point is justified by assumptions made in science and ordinary life. We thus would allow "the real" to supersede our conscious expressions of it by appealing to something in the historical event that lies beyond the subject-object relationship. Merely because an object cannot be known unless it is an object to some subject is no reason for supposing that it cannot exist apart from that subject. Croce never argued the truth of his presuppositions, so his conclusions give us reason for evaluating and perhaps revising them. His theory of judgment also failed to account for true and perhaps even false propositions derived from the use of an inductive method. And if true propositions occur, surely they are founded upon repeated observations, a community of agreement, and carefully weighed evidence. Croce moreover limited the application of "objective" to those true judgments that comprise theoretic disciplines such as philosophy, logic, and aesthetics. If we grant that true judgments occur in the empirical sciences, it would seem reasonable to describe them as being also objective.

Suppose that the cognitive act includes, directly or indirectly, an aspect not entirely the result of the expressive activity of mind. Let us acknowledge a characteristic of *epistemic* experience, whereby it transcends our intuitional and conceptual awareness. True judgment then would include more than our mental states. By recognizing a real relationship between an event and our knowledge of it—not simply the occurrence of conscious activities and their interrelations (in Croce's terms, "intuitional," "conceptual," "economic," or "ethical")—we would escape the problems that arise from his reduction of history and indeed philosophy itself to autobiography.

The Categorial Theory

Having discussed what I would discard in the Crocean philosophy, I would now like to consider what should be retained—that is, Croce's categorial theory of error. Besides his privation conception of purely theoretic errors of incoherence as outlined above, error also occurred whenever various subjects and predicates became misrepresented and the resulting judgment was claimed to be correct. Because this type of mistake falsified a relation that should hold between a representative (subject) and a category (predicate), I will refer to it as "categorial." Croce himself did not use this adjective. Indeed he never formally labeled this conception. I trust that the reasons for so naming it will become increasingly clear during the exposition of his doctrine. To put it briefly: my selection of "categorial" derived from a wish to differentiate this theory from Croce's coherence conception of true judgment. I wanted to indicate, moreover, that it depended upon his view of the relations between the categories of historical interpretation.

A categorial theory was unusual in a philosophy such as Croce's, since idealist systems frequently espoused some form of coherence conception only in determining true and false judgment. What was the historical antecedent for his view? Croce, as we saw in chapters 2 and 3, was influenced early in his career by Giambattista Vico's conceptions of art and history. Croce also adopted and developed Vico's notion of error "as an improper combination of ideas." [24] Categorial mistakes consisted thus of improperly substituting intuition or any other pseudoconcept for a category in judgment. They stemmed also from disrupting the organic unity between subject and predicate. Attempts to attribute logical or moral value to art and to deduce history from a priori concepts were included among Croce's examples of categorial mistakes.

Unlike the "negative" errors of coherence, categorial mistakes were "positive" and not purely theoretical. Positive error could not occur in the philosophic "sciences" as such, inasmuch as these disciplines expressed true judgments only. Such errors issued instead from one's practical activity, since they required the false affirmation that any combination of representation and category that served human short-term needs ("practical" goals) be true. By "practical" Croce intended to include not the ethical, but more simply the economic desire for personal gain. Categorial mistakes included prejudices of country, religion, class, and profession, along with deceptions based upon wishes to satisfy vanity and ambition.

The categorial mistakes that derived from practical acts were also fundamentally logical. For this reason Croce described them as theoretical-practical: "a fact like *humano capiti cervicem equinam jungere,* or *simulare cupressum* in the sea where the shipwrecked struggles in the waves, does not constitute . . . aesthetic error, unless there be added . . . a logical affirmation, so that the practical act becomes . . . logical error."[25] Yet a logically improper combination of ideas taken by itself was neither true nor false. As an illustration, the idea of a human head joined to a horse's neck could amount to an expression of pure fancy, a complex intuition. Intent to deceive one's self or others, which in the Crocean view required the *affirmation* that an incorrect combination of ideas be true, was a necessary prerequisite for categorial error. Unlike true judgments, such affirmations, which were acts of will for Croce, always included something of the contingent and arbitrary in them.

A limited number of improper combinations of intuition and concept could be deduced from the relations among the four kinds of human expression—intuitional, logical, economic, and ethical. Nevertheless one of Croce's major philosophic tasks was to refute the errors that derived from this source. Let us take a look at the varieties of categorial error that Croce listed.

Aestheticism, Empiricism, and Mathematicism

In judgment, the form of intuition was sometimes substituted for that of pure concept. A purely aesthetic proposition, however, was not expressed. In this case the value and function of the concrete-universal became attributed to an intuition-as-predicate, and one affirmed that the judgment was correct. Croce labeled these errors "aestheticism."

This epistemological view presupposed that *all* knowledge was intuitional and, moreover, that concrete-universals lacked universality and unity. Examples of such erroneous judgments were: "Intuition is the sole form of knowledge" and "Intuitions provide us with truth." Here queries as to whether one should evaluate art in terms of its "truth" amounted to treating intuition erroneously, as if it were a logical expression. In contemporary thought this notion has reappeared infrequently as "intuitionism" and the "philosophy of pure experience." [26]

"Empiricism" stemmed from judgments that incorrectly treated all concepts as if they were class names. This view did not distinguish between concrete-universals and pseudoconcepts. [27] A famous example lay in assertions formulated according to "literary kinds." [28] Criticism of aesthetic value became expressed in terms of criteria established for a particular art form. Such errors also appeared in the works of Auguste Comte. His nineteenth-century brand of French sociological thought (positivism) exemplified a confused commingling of various categories. Comte had based his speculations on empirical data and had confined philosophic method to classification. He judged historical events, thus, not in terms of activities of mind (intuitional, conceptual, economic, ethical) nor with the pure concepts that derived from these expressions of consciousness. Comte interpreted the past instead with arbitrary notions—for example, ancient, medieval, and modern periodicity. His sociological judgments such as "Human activity passes through the stages of offensive warfare, defensive warfare, and industry" erroneously substituted class names for concrete-universals, for example, development, art, theoretic and practical activity. Comte's assertions, moreover, attributed the function and value of the category to a pseudoconcept and affirmed that the resultant expression was true. [29]

Both "psychologism" and "neocriticism" were, in the Crocean view, variants of positivism. The former applied methods of induction and deduction to mental and moral sciences. Psychological aesthetics, for instance, was to include judgments that expressed empirical notions such as the sublime, the comic, and humor. These terms, however, belonged to descriptive psychology rather than to any philosophic discipline. [30] Neocriticism tended to eliminate every speculative tenet from

Kant's critique of reason. The followers of this approach developed theories founded upon the sciences or inductive metaphysics. Psychologism, neocriticism, and positivism committed the same category mistake. In judgment such doctrines substituted an empirical concept for a pure one, attributed the universality of a category to a "class term," and asserted that the statement was true.

Empiricism led to a dualism between appearance and essence. Induction postulated something "behind" phenomena. "Spiritism" (*spiritismo*) exemplified a futile attempt to determine the unknowable. This view erroneously supposed that all concepts were empirical and that no exhaustive inventory of the forms of consciousness can be rendered. For Croce, however, judgments about what could not be known were impossible, inasmuch as logical expression originated from intuition. Here the categorial error was identical with the positivistic ones of neocriticism and psychologism.

"Evolutionist positivism" occurred when empiricists endeavored to overcome the insufficiencies of their view.[31] In this case the supposedly antihistorical character of positivism was to be transcended. The attempt unfortunately amounted to a history of classification rather than "concrete history." Once again, arbitrary classes of various genera and species formed predicates in judgments that nevertheless were claimed as true.

"Rationalist positivism" also tried to correct the erroneous assumptions made by the empiricists.[32] Their tendency toward dualism and superstition was to be checked by faith in the absolute authority of thought. Reason's dependency upon empirical concepts, however, limited its application to series of arbitrary facts. Like the other forms of positivism, this one asserted that judgments formulated on practical grounds were true.

"Mathematicism" likewise originated from incorrect claims. One substituted an abstract term, such as "three" or "mathematical infinite," for a pure concept. These pseudoconcepts were believed to be historically concrete. The best illustrations of this categorial error did not occur in the works of the Pythagoreans, or in those of philosophers like Spinoza and Leibniz. Croce did not believe that these theoreticians were true mathematicians. One could find examples of this type of categorial error "in the unfulfilled programmes of such treatises and systems, or in the mathematicist treatments of certain philosophic problems." A similar mistake lay in the attempt to apply the mathematical concept "infinity" to historical reality. Croce took this term to mean the possibility of "always adding a unity to any number."[33] Mathematicism rested thus upon the claim that reality could be divided into separate "facts." But according to Croce reality was essentially an organic and continuous unity. Its fragmentation, however useful, amounted to a distortion of its character.

Categorial Errors Arising from Expediency

Aestheticism, empiricism, and mathematicism resulted from incorrectly combining intuition with concrete-universal, empirical, or abstract pseudoconcept. What other types of categorial error originated from disrupting the synthesis of judgment? Sometimes subject and predicate were associated for the sake of expediency. Historians formulated statements that were consistent with doctrine—for instance, of the "metaphysical" nature of history—and not with philological research. "Logism," "panlogism," "philosophism," and "philosophy of history" were the result of such erroneous assertions.[34] If philosophers interpreted documents, they then wrote history. If they speculated, the consequence was "philosophy of history." The most famous illustration of this mistake lay in Hegel's well-known work on history. Here whole civilizations were omitted in the Hegelian narrative of "world spirit."

"Philosophy of nature" likewise arose from disrupting the unity between representation and concept. The philosopher attempted *a priori* to deduce the pseudoconcepts of science. The content of scientific inquiry was, however, perception and history. This form of categorial error accordingly resolved itself into a theory of historical narrative, which treated subhuman reality. Other *Naturphilosophie* expressed a dilemma: either they simply continued the work of the physical and natural sciences or they deduced these disciplines *a priori*. Thought again interpreted representation in terms of preestablished doctrine, and facts became distorted. Among Croce's instances of erroneous judgments were:

1. The poles of the magnet are the opposed moments of the concept, made extrinsic and appearing in space.

2. Light is the ideality of nature.

3. Magnetism corresponds to length, elasticity to breadth, and gravity to volume.

4. Water, or fire, or sulphur, or mercury, is the essence of all natural facts.[35]

Such systems maintained, moreover, that there were contingent happenings that invariably defied rationalization: "nature in its self-externality is impotent to achieve the concept and the spirit."[36]

In judgment, when subject and predicate were disunited, an improper predicate (intuition) was posited, and the erroneous assertions that belong to "mythologism" occurred.[37] Intuitions were represented as concepts and predicated of one another. These expressions, however, formed, not propositions, but incorrect judgments, for like all category mistakes, myths claimed to be true. As examples, Croce gave the stories of Uranus and Gaea as well as the Prometheus tale. In such cases religion became mythology, and philosophy supposedly presented itself as true religion.

The Tendency toward Skepsis

The categorial errors I have mentioned tended toward "skepsis."[38] This theoretic position would correct the mistakes noted above and express an alternative view. If, however, skepsis should merely negate categorial errors, we would have "skepticism." In general the skeptics asserted that reality was an impenetrable mystery. They thus avoided the difficult labor of understanding consciousness and its expressions.

According to Crocean theory, "agnosticism" was a variant of skepticism and pertained to the "supreme principles of philosophy." This "posture" became a refuge for those who denied the validity of philosophic principles. Agnosticism included judgments that disengaged subject from predicate and implied that pure concepts were merely empirical. Indeed Croce stated that "agnostics and empiricists are ordinarily so closely connected that the one name is almost synonymous with the other."[39]

"Mysticism" represented another form of skepticism. This view held that, theoretically speaking, skeptics did not state the mystery that thought was unable to solve. As a form of error mysticism was, however, self-contradictory. It did not consistently affirm *any* thought. Croce put it this way: "To mysticism not even words can be permissible, because mysticism, being life and not contemplation, practice and not theory, is by definition *dumbness.*"[40]

Now that we have reviewed Croce's application of his categorial theory to various philosophic errors, let us look more closely at how it provided a useful tool for criticism, specifically, in aesthetics and historical narrative. Although it was suggestive in other inquiries as well, I have singled out these particular disciplines because it was here that Croce exercised his greatest influence on contemporary thought.

Croce's Categorial Theory: Its Contributions

A classical conception of literary form was based on what Croce deemed "a category mistake." This particular error rested on the affirmation that judgments combining representation with empirical concept (genre) were true. As we have seen, however, pseudojudgments were neither true nor false, merely relatively useful. What significance did Croce's categorial conception have for time-honored standards of art?

The genre that formerly had provided a *permanent ideal* for artistic creation became in Crocean aesthetics a *variable notion,* applied for practical and mnemonic purposes. Croce thus bluntly recommended analysis (in terms of the genre) of Shakespeare's art only for those who did not spontaneously feel. Arbitrary classifications of types of aesthetic expression served a merely didactic purpose and perhaps also softened "hard heads"—even those of educated men.[41]

Croce's revision of standards demonstrated his recognition of the tremendous variety of aesthetic expression. In the past, works that had not satisfied the criteria of "form" and "content" automatically met with derogatory judgment. As an example, Croce noted that for a long time the value of Shakespeare's art was contested or even negated. Tolstoy, for instance, complained that men did not speak in the mode of Shakespearean characters. Croce, however, countered that Tolstoy's personages and romances were more Shakespearean than "their great but only slightly reasonable and not at all critical author had thought."[42] Even a sense of "the classical" had been denied to Shakespeare—also by those who esteemed him. By this term critics understood "a one-sided and antiquated idea . . . that consisted of a definite external regularity." Shakespeare's work was nonetheless "classical" in the "authentic sense of expression," which for Croce meant unforced, continuous, moderate, and serene "poetry."[43]

Fruitless arguments that aestheticians, critics, and artists had waged could now be resolved with Croce's categorial theory. Such debates were based on judgments that confused the arbitrariness of a class name—for example, epic, tragedy, didactic poetry—with the universality of a pure concept—art. In his essay on Homer's work, Croce treated Aristotle's problem of whether "the epic" or "the tragedy" was the better form of imitation.[44] Croce resolved this dilemma (just as he had dealt with other problems based on definition of a genre) by translating it into relations between "the poetic" (art) and "the extra-poetic." Poetry, he concluded, was to be sought not in its structure, nor in its passages, but in the emotive quality that infused the entire expression. Every true lyric, according to Croce, represented the tragedy that pervaded life.[45] Other difficulties arose with attempts to classify art in terms of its design. The structures of Virgil's *Georgics,* for instance, has led critics to declare that the whole piece was "extra-poetic";[46] whereas for Croce, Virgil's description of nature was indeed poetry, even if it bordered on being didactic.

Croce's categorial conception of error likewise answered the question of whether a contemporary tragedy can be written. For literati such a question had turned on the fulfillment of the Aristotelian postulate of a fall from noble birth. In Crocean terms, however, these disputes neglected the task of the critic, which was not that of a "pork butcher" or "surgeon who carves away pieces of meat."[47] This conception of criticism was tantamount to evaluating art in terms of inflexible, unchanging rules. Rather, one was to determine that a lyrical and cosmic expression has occurred. By means of an elastic mode of recognizing artistic creation and its value, Croce sought to liberate art from the dogmatic restraints that the standards of "literary kinds" had imposed.

One of the most important of the genres was that of literature itself. Although it was given full prominence with the publication of Croce's *La poesia* in 1936,[48] when he was seventy years old, "literature" remained an arbitrary class name for him. In that work, however, it became characterized as resembling poetry, but as falling short of genuine lyrical and cosmic expression. The task of the critic, then, became one of distinguishing between literature and poetry. Nevertheless this differentiation did not mark a departure from Croce's earlier concept of criticism as determining the difference between non-art and art, but instead reaffirmed it. Croce's conception of art as lyrical and cosmic expression also remained unaltered. Here, however, in great detail and with many illustrations from his earlier critiques of the cosmic poets such as Dante, Ariosto, and Goethe, he described the differences between genuine poetic expression and the various forms of non-art, along with the relations that held among the latter. The practical classifications used in criticism were expressed via the pseudoconcepts as, for example, prosaic, literary, didactic, and oratorical forms. Thus every distinction within the practical sphere that had appeared in earlier works became restated and elaborated by use of an empirical method. His position was clear: there is "good literature," and at times non-poetic verse may be necessary in genuine poetry.

Thus Croce's writings from at least the publication of the *"Tesi fondamentali"* (1900) maintained that the classificatory use of the pseudoconcepts in literary criticism was indeed a practical necessity and served, moreover, a useful function. The critic, however, was to understand that these conceptual fictions did not possess the status of universal pure concepts and that the pseudojudgments formed from them were neither true nor false. They were to be altered or discarded depending upon the needs of the critic. Pseudojudgments amounted to didactic tools useful for interpretation and analysis. As such their expression was limited by the historical period and circumstances in which they were used.

Although Crocean aesthetics led some critics to revise their concepts, they did not always recognize his influence. For instance, in the essay "The Doctrine of Literary Forms," Roy Hack noted as a source for his ideas Henry Newbolt's book on the theory of forms.[49] Newbolt himself, however, had acknowledged his debt to Croce's critique of the genre. J. Craig La Drière still supported a theory of "literary kinds."[50] Joel Spingarn, on the other hand, agreed with Croce:

> We have done with the *genres,* or literary kinds. Their history is inseparably bound up with that of the classical rules. . . . But if art is organic expression, and every work of art is to be interrogated with the questions, "What has it expressed, and how completely?" there is no place for the question whether it has conformed to some convenient classification of critics or to some law derived from this classification.[51]

Probably Croce's influence on criticism derived as much from his attack on the genre as from any other one source. We have seen how his critique followed from his categorial conception of judgment. With its application, other questions that arise in aesthetics might also be settled. For instance, queries as to whether we should evaluate art in terms of its "truth" would amount to treating intuitional expression erroneously as if it were "logical."[52] Croce labeled such errors "aestheticism," a view claiming that intuition was the sole form of knowledge.[53] Likewise, judging art in terms of didactic effect involved confusing its theoretic nature with expressions of human practical activity. Marxist theories that would impose doctrinal standards (economic and "scientific") upon what is essentially alogical (intuition), moreover, also fell under Croce's categorial knife. Marxian aesthetics, thus, confused the relations that held among conscious activities. Finally, the problem of censorship, which presupposed that ethical criteria were applicable to art, became resolved. On the one hand, the *theoretic* essence of aesthetic creation lay in its lyrical, cosmic quality. Moral good, on the other hand, was expressed within the *practical* boundaries of political freedom.

We have seen the results of Croce's categorial theory when put to problems of aesthetics. What were its implications for historical narrative? Croce distinguished between so-called false pseudohistories and true accounts of the past. In a priori approaches to history, for instance, one improperly combined subject and predicate for practical purposes. Objects were made to agree with a preconceived theory of the general nature of history. The historian then attempted to deduce events a priori rather than in accordance with concrete occurrences. In this case one wrote narrative without confirmation by documents and endeavored to understand "the past" in terms of false analogies. Croce offered examples of these erroneous judgments: "The Middle Ages are the negation of ancient civilization"; "The modern epoch is the synthesis of these two opposites"; "Greece was thought and Rome action." [54]

Croce also applied his categorial theory to what he called "poetical history." This incorrect interpretation of events derived from an attempt to rectify the "barren" discoveries of philological treatises. Sentiment (intuition) overwhelmed critical thought. Aesthetic coherence became substituted for logical consistency. Examples occurred in historical biography, where the author's feelings dominated, or in the history of a country in which the historian vindicated events in accordance with political ideals:

> Numerous examples of this kind of history are afforded by the affectionate biographies of persons much beloved and venerated and by the satirical biographies of the detested; patriotic histories which vaunt the glory and lament the misadventures of the people to which the author belongs and with which he sympathizes, and those that shed a sinister light on the enemy people, adversary of his own. [55]

In this passage the genuine synthesis between representation and pure concept that was essential to true judgment has not taken place. The author has expressed instead mere feeling and poetry. Error occurred when purely aesthetic creations were claimed to be histories, for narrative issued not from emotion only, but from selective thought as well. To quote Croce:

if the divergence as to the concept arises from ignorance, prejudice, negligence, illegitimate private or national interests, and from other disturbing passions, that is to say, from *insufficient conceiving of the concepts*, or from inexact thought, the remedy is certainly not to be sought in the abandonment of concepts and of thought, but in correcting the former and making perfect the latter. Abandonment would not only be cowardly, but impossible. Having left the Eden of pure intuition and entered the field of history, it is not given us to retrace our steps.[56]

Poetical history, then, included the error described as "aestheticism." This category mistake occurred when intuition became substituted for concept, the function and characteristics of "the logical" were attributed to "the aesthetic," and the resultant judgment was proposed as correct.[57] For Croce, error lay not simply in the miscombined elements of judgment, but also in its truth claim. The phrase "poetical history" amounted to a contradiction in terms, since poetry could never be history.

A second application of Croce's categorial theory resulted in a critique of "praticistical history" described in earlier periods as "oratory." The judgments that comprised this kind of "narrative" were formulated for didactic purposes. In short, practicistical history was equivalent to rhetoric: it attempted to instruct or influence human actions rather than to interpret events. Genuine history, however, resulted from the theoretic activity of consciousness and was thus not couched in terms of any "extrinsic end":

> Hence rhetorical history (which would be more correctly termed *praticistical* history) is composed of two elements, history and the practical end, converging into one, which is the practical act. For this reason one cannot attack it, but only its theory.[58]

Croce also tested "universal history." Like all other pseudohistories, this variant included an unrealizable pretension—to "form a picture of all the things that have happened to the human race, from its origins upon the earth to the present moment. Indeed, it claims to do this from the origin of things, or the creation, to the end of the world, since it would not otherwise be truly universal."[59] The historian could never satisfy such a requirement. Universal narrative accordingly amounted to either chronicle (which Croce named "dead history") or poetry. In the first instance (chronicle), statements consisted of representation and pseudoconcept. A "true" judgment was not formed. In the second instance, no pure concept occurred but merely poetic expression took place.

What then did authentic historical inquiry involve for Croce? The historian was to solve specific problems and his response became limited by what he purported to treat. Universal histories thus must be transformed into "particular" ones.[60] Croce concluded that history was not entirely subjective (poetic), or purely universal (abstract), or merely practical. The subject of an investigation of the past was "the individual object," whereas the pure concepts that directed historical narrative represented what was concretely universal.[61] Much of history, like literary criticism, made use of conceptual fictions for purposes of classification and quantification. Again, such usage was indispensable for organization and communication. Categorial errors arose only when the historian asserted that such pseudojudgments correctly described events and objects and that narrative was formed exclusively of them.

What role did philosophy assume in relation to history? Early in his career Croce was influenced by Vico's notion that knowledge of the past fell within the province of philosophy.[62] Croce amended this conception by maintaining that, logically speaking, neither discipline was subordinate to the other. His theoretical change followed from the view that definition and individual judgment presupposed each other, much as pure concept became expressed via historical representation. In short, philosophy could not be resolved simply into history and, as we have seen, philosophy of history was based on a category mistake. Furthermore, neither history nor philosophy occurred without the other. On the one hand, historical narrative required categorial interpretation. On the other, philosophic categories and concepts necessarily presented themselves in historical contexts, providing thereby a framework in terms of which events and subjects were to be interpreted. Philosophy was to make explicit a priori categories of judgment used in historical narrative. This is what Croce had in mind when he described philosophy as the "methodological moment of historical narrative." Here I am in complete agreement with the Crocean conception of the relations that hold between philosophy and history.

Let us suppose, however, that we sever Croce's categorial theory from his idealist epistemology and theory of the phenomenological relations among activities of consciousness; indeed we must if we accept the realist position proposed earlier in this chapter. How, then, would we select the categories of historical interpretation? And what status would they possess? Through critical reflection on needs and interests, the historian would determine the interpretive categories for narrative. Although their selection would be made on pragmatic grounds, I would grant them a priori status inasmuch as they could not be falsified. Nevertheless they could be discarded when they no longer served a useful function.[63]

Did Croce's categorial conception of error itself suggest a theory of truth? And if so, then why did Croce not propose it? An obvious response would be that Croce was satisfied, on theoretic grounds at least, with his coherence theory. And in my opinion he accepted it unquestioningly along with the idealist epistemology with which it was joined. A second reply would be that whereas "truth" was a purely theoretic concept, categorial error amounted to a hybrid notion involving both theoretic and practical activities of human spirit. Thus, when considered from within the framework of Crocean phenomenology, this type of error could never imply any theory of *truth* as such. If, however, as I have proposed, we sever Croce's categorial theory from his idealist phenomenology, his theory of error then would be compatible with an empirical conception of verifiability. As I have argued above, the truth of particular judgments, such as "President Lincoln was assassinated by John Wilkes Booth," would depend upon empirical methods of direct and indirect verification. In this way their objectivity would be preserved.

My list of interpretive terms, moreover, would be broader than the one delineated by Croce's philosophy. It would include categories and their directive concepts drawn from empirical disciplines such as economics, sociology, demography, and psychology. An economic interpretation of the American Civil War, for instance, might be as viable as one in terms of the human struggle for greater political liberty, or of an Adlerian drive for power expressed in the debates between Lincoln and Douglas. In diverse narratives, religious concepts might predominate, for example, when treating the development of the present-day Libyan and Iranian states, or the contemporary Catholic rebellion in Ireland. In other cases, for instance, when discussing the evolution and interplay among art forms during the transition from French expressionism to impressionism, the category of art and aesthetic concepts might best suit the historian's needs.

The interpretive categories—economic, political, aesthetic, psychological, ethical, religious, and so forth—should remain distinct from one another. Thus, to evaluate an economic interpretation of events with aesthetic or ethical concepts would amount to a categorial error, and to interpret history of art in terms of economic and political concepts would be equally unsuitable. Accordingly, I would affirm the sort of mistake that arises when miscombining categories and directive concepts, or when trying to account for multifarious experience by appealing to one category only (sometimes described as "reductionism"). As I argued earlier, it seems indeed inevitable that experience will invariably transcend our attempts to categorize it. In agreement with Croce, then, I maintain that history does amount to histories, and the application of Crocean categorial theory in the ways outlined above does provide solutions to important philosophic problems in aesthetics, as well as in theory of history. We have seen that these resolutions include the status and function of the genre, the task of the critic, and the role of philosophy in its relation to history.

Notes

Chapter 1. Croce's Life
(pages 1−19)

1. For anyone who does not read Italian, Cecil Sprigge's *Benedetto Croce: Man and Thinker* (Cambridge, England: Bowes & Bowes, 1952; reprinted in Benedetto Croce, *Philosophy, Poetry, History,* trans. C. Sprigge [London: Oxford University Press, 1966]), provides the most detailed biography of Croce's life. Also see H. S. Harris, "Croce, Benedetto," *Encyclopedia of Philosophy* (New York: Macmillan, 1972); Gian N. G. Orsini, *Benedetto Croce: Philosopher of Art and Literary Critic* (Carbondale: Southern Illinois University Press, 1961), ch. 1; Angelo A. De Gennaro, *The Philosophy of Benedetto Croce* (New York: Russell & Russell, 1961); Raffaello Piccoli, *Benedetto Croce* (New York: Harcourt, Brace & Co., 1922); Giovanni Gullace's introduction to Benedetto Croce, *Poetry and Literature,* trans. G. Gullace (Carbondale: Southern Illinois University Press, 1981); and Edmund E. Jacobitti, *Revolutionary Humanism and Historicism in Modern Italy* (New Haven: Yale University Press, 1981). Croce's autobiographical statements that have been translated into English may be found in *Benedetto Croce: An Autobiography,* trans. R. G. Collingwood (Oxford: Clarendon Press, 1927); and Benedetto Croce, *My Philosophy and Other Essays on the Moral and Political Problems of Our Time,* selected by R. Klibansky, trans. E. F. Carritt (London: George Allen & Unwin, 1949), ch. 1.

2. Benedetto Croce, *Memorie della mia vita* (Napoli: Istituto italiano per gli studi storici, 1966), 10ff.

3. Fausto Nicolini, *Benedetto Croce* (Torino: Unione tipografico-editrice torinese, 1962), 67.

4. See Gilbert Murray, Manlio Brosio, and Guido Calogero, *Benedetto Croce* (London: Westerham Press, 1953), 36.

5. Robert Fulton, *Death and Identity* (New York: John Wiley, 1965), 259−72, 276ff.

6. Italo De Feo, *Benedetto Croce e il suo mondo* (Torino: Edizioni rai radiotelevisione italiana, 1966), 11.

7. Croce, *My Philosophy*, 133.

8. Nicolini, *Croce*, 39ff.

9. Croce, *Autobiography*, 35.

10. Sprigge, *Croce*, 78–79.

11. Croce, *Autobiography*, 37.

12. The descriptions of the relationship of the Spaventas to the Croce family have varied, perhaps due in part to the ambiguous meaning of *"cugini"* (cousins). See De Feo, *Croce*, 12, 15; Piccoli, *Croce*, 3, 4; and Sprigge, *Croce*, 12. However, according to Dr. Ernesto Paolozzi, reviewer for *La rivista di studi crociani* (Napoli), Silvio and Bertrando Spaventa were sons of Maria Croce, who was a sister of Croce's paternal grandfather. See *"Monterodomo: Storia di un comune e di due famiglie,"* in Benedetto Croce, *Storia del regno di Napoli* (Bari: Laterza, 1925).

13. Sprigge, *Croce*, 29–30.

14. Croce, *Memorie*, 12. My translation.

15. For an interesting discussion of adaptation to loss, see Martha Wolfenstein, *Disaster: A Psychological Essay* (Glencoe, Ill.: Free Press, 1957). By the same author see also "How Is Mourning Possible?" in *The Psychoanalytic Study of the Child* (New York: International Universities Press, 1966), 21:93–123, and "Loss, Rage, and Repetition," in *Psychoanalytic Study of the Child*, 24:457ff.

16. Croce, *Memorie*, 12–13. My translation.

17. Croce, *My Philosophy*, 240.

18. For a full bibliography of Croce's books, articles, and reviews published before 1960, see Silvano Borsari, *L'opera di Benedetto Croce* (Napoli: Istituto italiano per gli studi storici, 1963). For works and secondary sources published since 1960, consult L. M. Palmer and H. S. Harris, eds., *Thought, Action and Intuition* (New York: George Olms, 1975). Other selected bibliographies may be found in Orsini, *Croce;* Jacobitti, *Revolutionary Humanism;* and Croce, *Poetry and Literature*, trans. Gullace.

19. De Feo, *Benedetto Croce*, 7. My translation.

20. Sprigge, *Croce*, 10.

21. Croce, *Autobiography*, 92. For an insight into the intellectual exchange between Croce and Antonio Labriola, see the latter's *Lettere a Benedetto Croce* (Napoli: Istituto italiano per gli studi storici, 1975). Also see Benedetto Croce, *Materialismo storico ed economia marxistica*, 6th ed. rev. with appendix (Bari: Laterza, 1941), 265–306. (This reference was given to me by Dr. Ernesto Paolozzi.) Also see Raffaello Franchini, *Croce interprete di Hegel: e altri saggi filosofici* (Napoli: Giannini, 1964), 18ff.

22. Croce, *Autobiography*, 93.

23. This essay was reprinted in Croce's *Cultura e vita morale* (Bari: Laterza, 1914), 51–56.

24. This essay was reprinted in Croce's *Conversazioni critiche* (Bari: Laterza, 1918), 2:353–57.

25. Croce, *Autobiography*, 96, 97.

26. Benedetto Croce, *"Ciò che è vivo e ciò che è morto della filosofia di Hegel,"* *La critica: Rivista di letteratura, storia e filosofia* (Bari: Laterza) 4 (1906): 410–12.

27. Benedetto Croce, *Ciò che è vivo e ciò che è morto della filosofia di Hegel* (Bari: Laterza, 1907). The third edition of this work (1912) was translated into English as *What Is Living and What Is Dead of the Philosophy of Hegel*, trans. D. Ainslie (London: Macmillan & Co., 1915; New York: Russell & Russell, 1969). The 1907 book became incorporated in Croce's *Saggio sullo Hegel seguito da altri scritti di storia della filosofia* (Bari: Laterza: 1913), 3–148.

28. Croce, *My Philosophy*, 13.

29. Sprigge, *Croce*, 23.

30. See Croce, *Memorie*, 13.

31. De Feo, *Croce*, 17. My translation.

32. There appears to be some disagreement among authorities as to whether Labriola was a Marxist while Croce attended his lectures at the University of Rome. See, for instance, Pasquale Romanelli (Patrick Romanell), *The Philosophy of Giovanni Gentile* (New York: S. F. Vanni, 1938), 12; See also Carlo Antoni, *Commento a Croce* (Venezia: Pozzi, 1955), ch. 3, and Jacobitti, *Revolutionary Humanism*, 58. According to Dr. Ernesto Paolozzi, reviewer for the *Rivista di studi crociani* (Napoli), by 1885 Labriola was already a Marxist who corresponded with Engels and many leaders of international socialism, but he was a Marxist in a cultural and not in a political sense. On this distinction see Luigi Barzini, *From Caesar to the Mafia* (London: Hamish Hamilton, 1971), 115ff.

33. Croce, *Autobiography*, 51.

34. Benedetto Croce, *"La storia ridotto sotto il concetto generale dell'arte,"* *Atti dell'Accademia Pontaniana* 23:32. This essay was reprinted in Benedetto Croce, *Primi saggi* (Bari: Laterza, 1919; 3d ed., 1951), 1–46. For a discussion of *"La storia"* see ch. 3 of this work.

35. De Feo, *Croce*, 38. My translation.

36. Croce, *Autobiography*, 56ff.

37. Sprigge, *Croce*, 30. For a polemical discussion of Croce's concept of human economic activity, that is, of his concept of *vitalità* (vitality or vital force), see A. Parente, *"Intorno al concetto crociano di 'vitale': Storia e sostanza di un'interpretazione,"* in *Rivista di studi crociani* 8 (1971): 1–13; A. Bruno, *"Una lettera sul problema della vitalità,"* ibid., 283–86; and A. Parente, *"Riposta al Bruno sullo stesso tema,"* ibid., 287–97. Also see A. Bruno, *"L'estistenzialismo e la forma economica in Croce,"* *Historica* (1951), nos. 3–5; and by the same author *"Vitalità e dialettica nell'ultimo Croce,"* ibid. (1952), no. 3; *"La formazione crociana dei distinti e le ultime indagini sulla vitalità e la dialettica,"* in *Benedetto Croce*, ed. Francesco Flora (Milano: Malfasi, 1953), 107–28; *Economia ed etica nello*

svolgimento del pensiero crociano (Siracusa-Catania: Ciranna, 1958); *Metodologia e metafisica nel pensiero crociano* (Bologna: Leonardi, 1964); *La crisi dell'idealismo nell'ultimo Croce* (Bari: Laterza, 1964).

38. Benedetto Croce, *Materialismo storico ed economia marxistica* (Milano-Palermo: Sandron, 1900). For an English translation see Benedetto Croce, *Historical Materialism and the Economics of Karl Marx,* trans. C. M. Meredith (London: H. Latimer, 1914). For a comparatively recent treatment of Marx and Croce, see Manlio Ciardo, *Marx e Croce* (Napoli: Generoso Procaccini, 1983).

39. Croce, *Philosophy, Poetry, History,* 620.

40. Ibid., lx–lxi. Also see Jacobitti, *Revolutionary Humanism,* 3.

41. See Sprigge, *Croce,* 15ff.; De Gennaro, *Philosophy of Benedetto Croce,* 38; Romanelli, *Gentile,* 28ff.; Patrick Romanell, *Croce versus Gentile* (New York: S. F. Vanni, 1946); H. S. Harris, *The Social Philosophy of Giovanni Gentile* (Urbana: University of Illinois Press, 1960), 19ff.

42. Romanelli, *Gentile,* 20. Romanelli cites Genile's work, *Saggi critici,* 1st series (Napoli: Ricciardi, 1921), 11.

43. Sprigge, *Croce,* 16.

44. Giovanni Gentile, *Teoria generale dello spirito come atto puro* (Pisa: Mariotti, 1916). For an English translation see *The Theory of Mind as Pure act,* trans. from the 3d edition with an introduction by H. Wildon Carr (London: Macmillan, 1922).

45. Giovanni Gentile, *The Reform of Education,* trans. D. Bigongiari, with an introduction by B. Croce (New York: Harcourt, 1922).

46. See H. S. Harris, *Social Philosophy of Giovanni Gentile,* 221–23.

47. Benedetto Croce, *Estetica come scienza dell'espressione e linguistica generale* (Milano-Palermo-Napoli: Sandron, 1902). For an English translation see *Aesthetic as Science of Expression and General Linguistic,* trans. D. Ainslie (London: Macmillan, 1909). This translation was revised by Ainslie and republished in 1922 by Macmillan, but without the Heidelberg lecture that had been included in the 1909 edition. The 1922 version also presented all of part 2 ("History of Aesthetics") of the *Estetica,* which had been summarized in the 1909 work. In the pages that follow, unless otherwise indicated, I shall quote from the paperback edition of the 1922 *Aesthetic* (New York: Noonday Press, 1958).

48. The volume on logic was Benedetto Croce, *Logica come scienza del concetto puro,* 2d ed. rev. (Bari: Laterza, 1909). (The 1st edition of this work was entitled *"Lineamenti di una logica come scienza del concetto puro,"* *Atti dell'accademia pontaniana* 35 [1905]: 140.) The 2d edition was translated into English by D. Ainslie as *Logic as the Science of the Pure Concept* (London: Macmillan & Co., 1917). The volume on economics and ethics was Benedetto Croce, *Filosofia della pratica: Economia ed etica* (Bari: Laterza, 1909). Douglas Ainslie translated this work into English as *Philosophy of the Practical: Economic and Ethic* (London: Macmillan & Co., 1913). The historiography work was Benedetto Croce, *Teoria e storia della storiografia* (Bari: Laterza, 1917). The English translation of the

2d edition of this work was entitled *History: Its Theory and Practice,* trans. D. Ainslie (New York: Harcourt Brace & Co., 1921; republished, New York: Russell & Russell, 1960).

49. Benedetto Croce, *La filosofia di Giambattista Vico* (Bari: Laterza, 1911). This work was translated into English as *The Philosophy of Giambattista Vico,* trans. R. G. Collingwood (London: H. Latimer, 1913). Croce, *Filosofia di Hegel.*

50. Murray, Brosio, and Calogero, *Croce,* 32.

51. Ibid., 25.

52. Sprigge, *Croce,* 18.

53. Ibid., 62.

54. Denis M. Smith, *Mussolini* (New York: Knopf, 1982), 147.

55. Murray, Brosio, and Calogero, *Croce,* 34−35.

56. Ibid., 35.

57. *Quaderni della "Critica"* (Bari: Laterza, 1945−51).

58. *Rinascita: Rassegna di politica e di cultura italiana* (Roma). For an excellent discussion of the relations between Croce and contemporary Italian communism, see Antonio Jannazzo, *Croce e il comunismo* (Napoli: Edizioni scientifiche italiane, 1982).

Chapter 2. An Outline of the Crocean Philosophy
(pages 20−33)

1. Croce, *My Philosophy,* 11.

2. Ibid., 15.

3. See Benedetto Croce, *"Biografia che è storia e biografia che è psicologia,"* La critica 31 (1933): 397. My translation.

4. Croce, *Autobiography,* 19ff. Also see Benedetto Croce, *History: Its Theory and Practice,* 151.

5. Croce, *My Philosophy,* 20.

6. See M. E. Moss, "Croce's Theory of Intuition Reconsidered," *La rivista di studi crociani* 15 (1978): 292−306.

7. See Paul Carus's treatment of Croce's use of the term "intuition" in "Croce's Use of the Word 'Intuition,'" *The Monist* 26 (Chicago: Open Court, 1916): 312−15; and Bernard Bosanquet's *Three Lectures on Aesthetic* (London: Macmillan & Co., 1915), 67ff.

8. Benedetto Croce, *"Estetica e psicologia del linguaggio,"* La critica 5 (1907): 412−13. My translation.

9. Benedetto Croce, *Aesthetic* (1958), 4.

10. Benedetto Croce, *Guide to Aesthetics,* trans. Patrick Romanell (Indianapolis: Bobbs-Merrill, 1965), 27.

11. Croce distinguished between the *fantasia,* which functioned creatively, and the *immaginazione,* which merely mechanically combined images. See B. Croce, *"Fantasia e*

immaginazione," Quaderni 6 (1949): 117. Also see L. M. Palmer and H. S. Harris, eds., *Thought, Action and Intuition*, 49–50.

12. Benedetto Croce, *Ariosto, Shakespeare e Corneille* (Bari: Laterza, 1968), 170. My translation. Cf. Benedetto Croce, *Ariosto, Shakespeare and Corneille*, trans. Douglas Ainslie (New York: Russell & Russell, 1966), 295.

13. See Croce, *Aesthetic* (1909).

14. Croce, *Aesthetic* (1958), 61.

15. B. Croce, *"La disputa intorno all'arte pura' e la storia dell'Estetica,"* *La critica* 32 (1934): 87.

16. Croce, *Philosophy, Poetry, History*, 82.

17. Croce, *Logic*, 37–38. Also see 19ff.

18. Ibid., 26.

19. Croce, *Philosophy of the Practical*, 312–13.

20. Croce, *My Philosophy*, 29–30.

21. Benedetto Croce, *The Defence of Poetry*, trans. E. F. Carritt (London: Oxford, 1933), 28. This work, consisting of the Philip Maurice Deneke Lecture, delivered at Lady Margaret Hall, Oxford, 1933, was published first in English and subsequently in Italian under the title *"Difesa della poesia,"* *La critica* 32 (1934): 1–15.

22. Ibid., 28.

23. De Feo, *Croce*, 90. My translation.

24. Croce, *My Philosophy*, 11.

Chapter 3. The Sphere of the Aesthetic
(pages 34–58)

1. Edmondo Cione, *Benedetto Croce* (Milano: Longanesi & Co., 1935); Cosimo Gancitano, *Critica dell'estetica crociana* (Marzara: Società editrice siciliana, 1948); and Orsini, *Croce*. Also see Giovanni Castellano, *Benedetto Croce* (Bari: Gius. Laterza & Figli, 1936).

2. Benedetto Croce, *"L'intuizione pura e il carattere lirico dell'arte,"* reprinted as an essay in *Problemi di estetica* (Bari: Laterza & Figli, 1954), 3–30. The essay was published first as an article in *La critica* 6 (1908): 321–40. It was translated into English by D. Ainslie and appears in his 1909 edition of the *Aesthetic*, but not in subsequent revised editions.

3. Benedetto Croce, *"Il carattere di totalità dell'espressione artistica,"* *Nuovi saggi* (Bari: Laterza & Figli, 1958), 119–46. This essay was translated into English by C. Sprigge and appears in *Philosophy, Poetry, History*, 261–73. *"Il caratere di totalità"* was published first as an article in *La critica* 16 (1918): 129–40.

4. Croce, *Primi saggi*, 23–24, n. 1. My translation.

5. In the section of *Primi saggi* entitled *"Illustrazioni e discussioni"* and dated 1895

(two years later than *"La storia"*), Croce noted that an affirmation of the cognitive nature of art lay at the foundation of Vico's thought (ibid., 65). Subsequently, in a 1901 paper that was reprinted in the 1902 *Estetica*, Croce described Vico as "the real revolutionary who . . . actually discovered the true nature of poetry and art and, so to speak, invented the science of Aesthetic" (Croce, *Aesthetic* [1958], 220). He, before anyone else, had recognized the autonomy of aesthetic expression as a creative activity of the human spirit (Croce, *Estetica* [1958], 242–58, and Croce, *Aesthetic* [1958], 220–34). Also see Benedetto Croce, *"Giambattista Vico primo scopritore della scienza estetica," Flegrea,* 3d year, 2 (1901): 1–26, 97–116.

6. Croce, *Autobiography,* 78–79.

7. Croce, *Memorie,* 16. My translation.

8. Pasquale Villari, a professor at the University of Florence, had been a student of De Sanctis. See Pasquale Villari, *"La storia è una scienza?" Nuova antologia* (Feb. 16, April 16, July 16, 1891). At one time apparently Croce held the opposite view—that history was indeed a science. See D. Ainslie's introduction to *Aesthetic* (1909), xxii.

9. The Italian reaction against positivism was directed specifically toward Spencer, Ardigò, and Lombroso. See Romanelli, *Gentile,* 4ff.

10. Croce, *Primi saggi,* 61.

11. See, for instance, De Gennaro, *Croce,* 24. Croce's *Breviario di estetica: Quattro lezioni* (Bari: Laterza, 1913) was translated by D. Ainslie and published first in English under the title "The Breviary of Aesthetic," *The Book of the Opening of the Rice Institute* (Houston: The Rice Institute, 1912), 2:450–517. This translation was subsequently revised and republished under the title *The Essence of Aesthetic* (London: Heinemann, 1921). More recently the *Breviario* was retranslated by Patrick Romanell under the title *Guide to Aesthetics* (Indianapolis: Bobbs-Merrill, 1965).

12. Croce, *Primi saggi,* 12, 13, 35, 36.

13. Ibid., 16ff, 23.

14. Ibid., 61. (Also see A. G. Baumgarten, *Aesthetica,* 2 vols. [*Frankfurt an der Oder,* 1750–58]).

15. Ibid., 35, 36.

16. Ibid., ix–x. A mature Croce was able to estimate both positive and negative effects of positivism. The former included an emphasis on method and antimetaphysical approach to philosophy. See Romanelli, *Gentile,* 21, ch. 1.

17. Croce, *"Lineamenti di una logica,"* 140.

18. Benedetto Croce, *"Tesi fondamentali di un'estetica come scienza dell'espressione e linguistica generale," Atti dell'accademia pontaniana* 30 (1900): 88.

19. Apparently Giosuè Carducci's work had profoundly influenced Croce at the *liceo.* Only later and gradually did he come to understand the significance of De Sanctis's view. See Croce, *Autobiography,* 78ff., and Jacobitti, *Revolutionary Humanism,* 47, 96ff.

20. Croce, *Autobiography,* 63.

21. Croce, *Estetica* (1958), 6. My translation. Cf. Croce, *Aesthetic* (1958), 4.

22. Croce, *Aesthetic* (1958), 28.

23. Croce, *Estetica* (1958), 31. My translation. Cf. Croce, *Aesthetic* (1958), 27.

24. Croce, *Aesthetic* (1958), 29.

25. Ibid., 28.

26. Ibid., 11.

27. Croce *Autobiography,* 95.

28. Croce, *Aesthetic* (1958), 221.

29. Ibid., 13.

30. Ibid., 20.

31. See Benedetto Croce, *The Poetry of Dante,* trans. D. Ainslie (New York: Paul P. Appel, 1971).

32. Croce, *Autobiography,* 104. Also see B. Croce, *"Intuizione, sentimento, liricità,"* La critica 5 (1907): 248.

33. Orsini, *Croce,* 324, n. 1.

34. Giulio A. Levi, *Studi estetici* (Lapi: Città di castello, 1907) 170.

35. Croce, *"Intuizione,"* La critica 5 (1907): 248.

36. Croce, *Autobiography,* 102.

37. Croce, *"L'intuizione pura,"* Problemi di estetica, 3–11.

38. Ibid., 12ff.

39. Ibid., 22.

40. Ibid., 17. My translation.

41. Croce, *Guide to Aesthetics,* 32.

42. Croce, *Nuovi saggi,* 119. My translation. Cf. Croce, *Philosophy, Poetry, History,* 261.

43. Croce, *Philosophy, Poetry, History,* 263.

44. Ibid., 269.

45. See Joel Spingarn's review of Croce's *Estetica* in *Nation* 75 (Sept. 25, 1902): 252–53.

46. Croce, *Philosophy, Poetry, History,* 261–262.

47. Croce, *Defence of Poetry,* 25ff.

48. Croce, *Ariosto, Shakespeare e Corneille,* 87. My translation. Cf. Croce, *Ariosto, Shakespeare and Corneille,* 146.

49. For alternative interpretations, cf. Cione, *Croce,* 63–64; Gancitano, *Critica dell'estetica crociana,* 36.

50. See Castellano, *Croce,* 37.

51. See Gancitano, *Critica dell'estetica crociana,* 36.

52. Orsini, *Croce,* 210ff.

53. We should recall that for Croce, art was intuitional expression of images, organically synthesized to form a particular feeling, whereas the material artifact, usually believed to form a part of the aesthetic work, became categorized as the product of practical activity (will). An art critic was, thus, also an artist. Upon stimulation by an ar-

tifact, he reproduced, or rather created, a work of art (complex aesthetic image) in his "*fantasia.*"

54. Orsini, *Croce*, 224–25.

55. See ibid., 36, on this point.

56. See ibid., 213, 215–16 on this point.

57. Benedetto Croce, *Ultimi saggi* (Bari: Gius. Laterza & Figli, 1963), 54–57.

58. Croce, *Guide to Aesthetics*, 15, 32, 44.

59. Croce, *Nuovi saggi*, 16. My translation. Cf. Croce, *Guide to Aesthetics*, 15.

60. Croce, *Nuovi saggi*, 122. My translation. Cf. Croce, *Philosophy, Poetry, History*, 263.

61. Croce, *Nuovi saggi*, 124. My translation. Cf. Croce, *Philosophy, Poetry, History*, 265. See also Carlo Antoni, *Commento a Croce*, 95, 96.

62. For a discussion of this point, see M. M. Milburn, "Benedetto Croce's Coherence Theory of Truth," *Filosofia* (Torino, Nov. 1968), 107–16.

63. Croce, *Guide to Aesthetics*, 5.

Chapter 4. The Sphere of Logic
(pages 59–82)

1. For a critique of Croce's logic of philosophy see Guido Calogero's *Logica, gnoseologia, ontologia* (Torino: Einaudi, 1948), 167ff.

2. For a discussion of the Crocean concept as representing a reformation of the Hegelian concrete-universal and thus a return to the Kantian category, see Francesco Valentini's *La controriforma della dialettica* (Roma: Riuniti, 1966).

3. On relations between Croce and Hegel, see L. Scaravelli, *Critica del capire* (Firenze, 1942); D. Faucci, *Storicismo e metafisica nel pensiero crociano* (Firenze: La nuova italia, 1950); R. Franchini, *Esperienza dello storicismo* (Napoli: Giannini, 1964) and *Croce interprete di Hegel* (Napoli: Giannini, 1964); G. Sasso, *Benedetto Croce: La ricerca della dialettica* (Napoli: Morano, 1975).

4. I wish to acknowledge Dr. Ernesto Paolozzi's helpful suggestions for interpreting the Crocean concept.

5. Croce, *Autobiography*, 52.

6. Giambattista Vico, *The New Science of Giambattista Vico*, trans. T. G. Bergin and M. H. Fisch (Ithaca: Cornell University Press, 1970).

7. Benedetto Croce, *La critica letteraria. Questioni teoriche* (Roma: Loescher, 1894). This work was republished in the *Primi saggi*, 75–168.

8. Croce, *Autobiography*, 55.

9. See Croce, *Historical Materialism and the Economics of Karl Marx*.

10. Croce, *Autobiography*, 58.

11. Ibid., 82–83.

12. Croce, *Aesthetic* (1958), 70.

13. See Antoni, *Commento a Croce*.

14. Croce, *Filosofia di Hegel* (1907), 5–7. My translation. Cf. Croce, *Philosophy of Hegel* (1915, 1969), 5–7.

15. Croce, *My Philosophy*, 15.

16. Benedetto Croce, *The Conduct of Life*, trans. Arthur Livingston (New York: Harcourt, Brace & Co., 1924; Freeport, N.Y.: Books for Libraries Press, 1967), 159–60. The work contains essays that began appearing in *La critica* in 1915 under the title "Frammenti di etica" (Fragments of ethics), a title that was intended to convey Croce's problematic approach to philosophy.

17. Croce, *Logic*, 92–93.

18. See Croce's *Philosophy of Hegel* (1969), chs. 4, 5.

19. Croce, *Filosofia di Hegel*, 89, ch. 4. My translation. Cf. *Philosophy of Hegel*, 91, ch. 4.

20. Croce, *Philosophy, Poetry, History*, 52.

21. Croce, *My Philosophy*, 18.

22. Croce, *Philosophy, Poetry, History*, 82.

23. Croce, *Filosofia di Hegel*, 86–88, ch. 4. My translation. Cf. *Philosophy of Hegel*, 88–89, ch. 4.

24. See Jacobitti, *Revolutionary Humanism*, 137ff.

25. Croce, *Filosofia di Hegel*, 114, ch. 6. My translation. *Philosophy of Hegel*, 120.

26. Croce, *Filosofia di Hegel*, 124, ch. 6. My translation. Cf. *Philosophy of Hegel*, 129.

27. Croce, *Indagini su Hegel*, 142. My translation.

28. Croce, "Il sentimento shakespeariano," in *Ariosto, Shakespeare e Corneille*, 86. My translation. Cf. "Shakespearean Sentiment," in *Ariosto, Shakespeare and Corneille*, 143. Croce did acknowledge that for Shakespeare goodness or virtue as such was stronger than evil, but not because the latter became resolved or assimilated into the former. Virtue was more powerful than evil simply because of its quality as virtue. Nevertheless evil was a fully real force and in this respect was as "strong" as goodness.

29. Croce, *Indagini su Hegel*, 141–42.

30. Ibid., 142.

31. For a discussion of Croce's categorial theory, see M. E. Moss, "The Enduring Values in the Philosophy of Benedetto Croce," *Idealistic Studies* 10 (Jan. 1980): 46–66. Also see Ernesto Paolozzi's review of this article in the *Rivista di studi crociani* 17 (July–Sept. 1980): 299–301.

32. Croce, *Logic*, 208.

33. Ibid., 112.

34. Ibid., 114–15.

35. Ibid., 116.

36. Ibid., 170.

37. Ibid., 177.

38. Croce, *Aesthetic* (1958), 4–5.

39. Croce, *Logic*, 197.

40. Croce, *Logica*, 127–28. My translation. Cf. *Logic*, 199.

41. Croce, *Logica*, 131–32. Cf. *Logic*, 204–5.

42. Croce, *Logic*, 218; also see 114–15, 205, 220–21, 224–25.

43. See, for instance, Jacobitti, *Revolutionary Humanism*, 137–39.

44. Croce, *Logic*, 180.

45. Ibid., 188–91.

46. Ibid., 181, 185ff.

47. Ibid., 186.

48. Ibid., 191–94.

Chapter 5. Truth and Error
(pages 83–112)

1. For a discussion of Croce's coherence theory see M. M. Milburn, "Benedetto Croce's Coherence Theory of Truth: A Critical Evaluation," *Filosofia* 19 (1968): 107–16. Also see Croce, *Logic*, 391ff.

2. Benedetto Croce, *History of Europe in the Nineteenth Century*, trans. Henry Furst (New York: Harcourt, Brace & Co., 1933), 362. The first Italian edition was entitled *Storia d'Europa nel secolo decimonono* (Bari: Laterza, 1932). Also see A. R. Caponigri, *History and Liberty* (London: Routledge and Kegan Paul, 1955), 169ff., for a discussion of this work and of Croce's "perspectivism."

3. Croce, *History: Its Theory and Practice*, 91.

4. Croce, *My Philosophy*, 20. Also see B. Croce, *"L'immaterialismo del Berkeley,"* La *critica* 7 (1909): 78.

5. Croce, *History: Its Theory and Practice*, 91.

6. Maurice Mandelbaum, *The Problem of Historical Knowledge* (New York: Liveright, 1938), 56.

7. Croce, *Logic*, 268.

8. Croce, *"Della possibilità e dei límiti del giudizio estetica,"* republished in the *Primi saggi*, 97, 103. My translation.

9. Ibid., 104, 105, 107. My translation.

10. Croce, *Aesthetic* (1958), 122, 123.

11. For a discussion of the critic's want of "self-consistency," see A. B. Walkley, *Dramatic Criticism* (London: John Murray, 1903), 72ff.

12. Croce, *Aesthetic* (1958), 125–26.

13. Croce, *History: Its Theory and Practice*, 21ff, also see 17–19.

14. Benedetto Croce, *Aesthetica in nuce* (Napoli: Cooperativa tipografica sanitaria, 1929). Also see "Aesthetic," in the *Encyclopaedia Britannica*, 14th ed. (1929). "Aesthet-

ica" (the Italian version) was reprinted in the *Ultimi saggi*, 3–43, and "Aesthetic" (the English version) in *Philosophy, Poetry, History*, 215–47.

15. Croce, *History: Its Theory and Practice*, 29.

16. Ibid., 136.

17. Croce, *Logic*, 302.

18. Ibid., 301–2.

19. Croce, *Nuovi saggi*, 79. My translation. Cf. *Guide to Aesthetics*, 73.

20. For an excellent discussion of objectivity in narrative see Maurice Mandelbaum, *The Anatomy of Historical Knowledge* (Baltimore: Johns Hopkins University Press, 1977), part 3.

21. See, for example, Croce, "*Lo storicismo*,"*Quaderni* 5(13)(Mar. 1949): 83. Here and elsewhere, Croce used "historicism" to denote his view of history as the treatment of distinct problems.

22. Croce, *History: Its Theory and Practice*, 12.

23. B. Croce, "*Postille*,"*La critica* 26(1928): 231–32. My translation. Also see Croce, *History: Its Theory and Practice*, 11ff.

24. Piccoli, *Croce*, 117–18. Also see Croce, *Logic*, 397.

25. Croce, *Logic*, 398. Also see *Logica*, 257. In the ninth Italian edition (1964), the Latin phrases "*humano capiti cervicem equinam jungere*," and "*simulare cupressum*" do not appear. The text reads instead: "*L'atto di congiungere al capo umano la cervice equina o dipingere il cipresso in mezzo al mare . . . .*" (The act of joining a horse's neck to a human head or representing a cypress in the midst of the sea).

26. Croce, *Logic*, 406–7.

27. Ibid., 407ff.

28. B. Croce, "*Postilla alla lettera di R. Eisler*," *La critica* 3 (1905): 86ff.

29. Croce, *Logic*, 408–11.

30. B. Croce, "*Antiestetica ed antifilosofia*,"*La critica* 1 (1903): 317. Also see B. Croce, "*La teoria del comico*," *La critica* 32 (1934): 204, 208.

31. Croce, *Logic*, 413–14.

32. Ibid., 414.

33. Ibid., 401, 406, 415–17.

34. Ibid., 420–26 (cf. *Logica*, 271ff).

35. Ibid., 429–32.

36. Ibid., 433.

37. Ibid., 438ff.

38. Ibid., 447ff.

39. Ibid., 455.

40. Ibid., 456.

41. Croce, *Ariosto, Shakespeare e Corneille*, 164; cf. *Ariosto, Shakespeare and Corneille*, 283.

42. Croce, *Ariosto, Shakespeare e Corneille*, 164–65; cf. *Ariosto, Shakespeare and Corneille*, 284–86.

43. Croce, *Ariosto, Shakespeare e Corneille,* 168; cf. *Ariosto, Shakespeare and Corneille,* 290–91.

44. See Benedetto Croce, *"Omero,"* in *Poesia antica e moderna: Interpretazioni* (Bari: Laterza, 1966), 31–38. This essay was translated into English by Cecil Sprigge. See Croce, "Homer in the Criticism of Antiquity," in *Philosophy, Poetry, History,* 769–75.

45. Croce, *Poesia antica e moderna,* 31–32; cf. *Philosophy, Poetry, History,* 769–70.

46. Croce, *Poesia antica e moderna,* 49.

47. Ibid., 154; cf. *Philosophy, Poetry, History,* 825.

48. Benedetto Croce, *La poesia: Introduzione alla critica e storia della poesia e della letteratura* (Bari: Laterza, 1963). For an English translation, see Benedetto Croce, *Poetry and Literature,* trans. Giovanni Gullace (Carbondale: Southern Illinois University Press, 1981).

49. Roy Kenneth Hack, "The Doctrine of Literary Forms," *Harvard Studies in Classical Philology,* ed. Committee of the Classical Instructors of Harvard University (Cambridge: Harvard University Press, 1916), 38: 1–65. Also see Sir Henry Newbolt, *New Study of English Poetry* (London: Constable and Co., Ltd., 1917).

50. See. J. Craig La Drière "Classifications of Literature," *Dictionary of World Literature: Criticism, Forms, Technique,* ed. Joseph T. Shipley. Rev. ed. (New York: Philosophical Library, 1953), 62–64. Also see Orsini, *Croce,* 339–40, n. 17.

51. J. E. Spingarn, *Creative Criticism* (New York: Henry Holt & Co., 1917), 26–27.

52. For a comparison between Croce and Coleridge, see G. N. G. Orsini and B. T. Gates, "The Quest for Aesthetic Truth," in *Thought, Action and Intuition,* ed. Palmer and Harris, 266ff.

53. Croce, *Logic,* 406–411.

54. Ibid., 425–26.

55. Croce, *History: Its Theory and Practice,* 35.

56. Croce, *Logic,* 291.

57. Ibid., 406–7.

58. Croce, *History: Its Theory and Practice,* 42.

59. Ibid., 56.

60. For a critique of the attempt to formulate a universal history, which, however, issues from a foundation diverse from Croce's idealist one, see Maurice Mandelbaum, "The History of Philosophy: Some Methodological Issues," *Journal of Philosophy* 74 (no. 10, Oct. 1977): 561–72.

61. B. Croce, *"La storiografia letteraria e artistica,"* *La critica* 27 (1929): 86–87.

22. See Max H. Fisch, "Croce and Vico" and L. M. Palmer, "Reflections on M. Fisch's 'Croce and Vico,'" in *Thought, Action and Intuition,* ed. Palmer and Harris, 184–240.

63. See C. I. Lewis, *Mind and the World Order* (New York: Dover, 1956), chs. 3, 8, and 11.

Selected Bibliography

The most complete bibliography of Croce's works has been compiled by Silvano Borsari in *L'opera di Benedetto Croce* (Napoli: Istituto italiano per gli studi storici, 1963). An excellent but less detailed bibliography is given in Fausto Nicolini's *L' "editio ne varietur" delle opere di B. Croce: Saggio bibliografico con taluni riassunti o passi testuali e ventinove fuori testo* (Napoli: Biblioteca del "Bollettino" dell'archivio storico del Banco di Napoli, 1960). For secondary works and articles written before 1942, see Edmondo Cione, *Bibliografia crociana* (Torino: Fratelli Bocca, 1956). For secondary works and articles written after 1960, see the bibliography appended to *Thought, Action and Intuition*, ed. L. M. Palmer and H. S. Harris (New York: George Olms, 1975). My bibliography has been selected from Croce's theoretical writings in the disciplines of logic, history-philosophy, and aesthetics, as well as from his practical writings, which help to clarify the former by way of example. I composed the list of English and Italian secondary sources according to the same criteria. The bibliography cites the dates of the editions quoted throughout the text.

Croce's Writings

1. BOOKS AND ARTICLES

"Aesthetics." In *Encyclopaedia Britannica.* 14th ed., 1929: 263–72. Reprinted in English under the same title, in *Philosophy, Poetry, History*, 215–47, and in Italian under the title *"Aesthetica in nuce,"* in *Ultimi saggi*, 3–43.

"Antiestetica ed antifilosofia." La critica: rivista di letteratura, storia e filosofia 1 (1903): 316–20. Reprinted in *Problemi di estetica*, 471–77.

Ariosto, Shakespeare e Corneille. 1st economic reprint of 5th ed. Bari: Laterza, 1968. Translated by D. Ainslie under the title *Ariosto, Shakespeare and Corneille.* New York: Russell & Russell, 1966. The essays *"Persona pratica e persona poetica"* and *"La tragedia della volontà"* were translated also by C. Sprigge in *Philosophy, Poetry, History,* 886–99.

"Biografia che è storia e biografia che è psicologia." La critica: Rivista di letteratura, storia e filosofia 31 (1933): 397–99. Reprinted in *Conversazioni critiche,* 5th series, 199–201.

Breviario di estetica: Quattro lezioni. Bari: Laterza, 1913. Translated by D. Ainslie and published first in English under the title "The Breviary of Aesthetic." *The Book of the Opening of the Rice Institute.* Houston: The Rice Institute 2 (1912): 450–517. This translation was subsequently revised and republished under the title *The Essence of Aesthetic.* London: Heinemann, 1921. More recently the *Breviario* was retranslated by Patrick Romanell under the title *Guide to Aesthetics.* Indianapolis: Bobbs-Merrill, 1965.

Il carattere della filosofia moderna. 3d ed. Bari: Laterza, 1963.

"Il carattere di totalità della espressione artistica." La critica: Rivista di letteratura, storia e filosofia 16 (1918): 129–40. Reprinted in *Nuovi saggi di estetica,* 117–46. This essay was translated by C. Sprigge under the title "The Totality of Artistic Expression" in *Philosophy, Poetry, History,* 261–73.

"Ciò che è vivo e ciò che è morto della filosofia di Hegel." La critica: Rivista di letteratura, storia e filosofia 4 (1906): 410–12.

Ciò che è vivo e ciò che è morto della filosofia di Hegel: Studio critico seguito da un saggio di bibliografia hegeliana. Bari: Laterza, 1907. Reprinted without the bibliography in *Saggio sullo Hegel seguito da altri scritti di storia della filosofia.* 5th ed. Bari: Laterza, 1967. The 3d edition of *Filosofia di Hegel* (1912) was translated into English by D. Ainslie under the title *What Is Living and What Is Dead of the Philosophy of Hegel.* New York: Russell & Russell, 1969.

"Contributo alla critica di me stesso." In *Etica e politica,* 375–423. This essay was translated into English by R. G. Collingwood, with a preface by J. A. Smith, under the title *Benedetto Croce: An Autobiography.* Oxford: Clarendon Press, 1927.

Conversazioni critiche. 4th rev. ed. of 1st and 2d series. Bari: Laterza, 1950.

Conversazioni critiche. 2d ed. rev. of 3d, 4th, and 5th series. Bari: Laterza, 1951.

"La critica e la storia delle arti figurative e le sue condizioni presenti." La critica: Rivista di letteratura, storia e filosofia 17 (1919): 265–78. Reprinted in *Nuovi saggi di estetica,* 259–85.

La critica letteraria: Questioni teoriche. Roma: Loescher, 1894. Reprinted in the *Primi saggi,* 73–168.

Cultura e vita morale. 3d ed. Bari: Laterza, 1955.

"Difesa della poesia." La critica: Rivista di letteratura, storia e filosofia 32 (1934): 1–15. Reprinted in *Ultimi saggi,* 61–81. This essay was published first in English under the title *The Defence of Poetry: Variations on the Theme of Shelley,* trans. E. F. Carritt. Oxford: Clarendon Press, 1933.

Discorsi di varia filosofia. 2d ed. 2 vols. Bari: Laterza, 1959.

Estetica come scienza dell'espressione e linguistica generale. 10th ed. Bari: Laterza, 1958. This work was translated into English under the title *Aesthetic as Science of Expression and General Linguistic,* trans. D. Ainslie. London: Macmillan & Co., 1909. The *Aesthetic* (1909) was revised in the 2d edition (1922) but did not include the essay "Pure Intuition and the Lyrical Character of Art." See *Aesthetic as Science of Expression and General Linguistic.* New York: Noonday Press, 1958.

"Estetica e psicologia del linguaggio." La critica: Rivista di letteratura, storia e filosofia 5 (1907): 411–13. Reprinted in *Problemi di estetica,* 186–90.

Etica e politica. 4th ed. Bari: Laterza, 1956.

"Fantasia e immaginazione." Quaderni dell "critica" 15 (1949): 117. Reprinted in *Terza pagine sparse,* 2 : 163–64.

Filosofia della pratica: Economica ed etica. 8th ed. Bari: Laterza, 1957. Translated by D. Ainslie under the title *Philosophy of the Practical: Economic and Ethic.* New York: Biblo and Tannen, 1967.

La filosofia di G. B. Vico. 3d economic reprint of 6th ed. Bari: Laterza, 1973. Translated by R. G. Collingwood under the title *The Philosophy of Giambattista Vico.* New York: Russell and Russell, 1964.

Filosofia e storiografia. 2d ed. Bari: Laterza, 1969.

Filosofia, poesia, storia. Milano-Napoli: Ricciardi, 1951. Translated by C. Sprigge under the title *Philosophy, Poetry, History.* London: Oxford University Press, 1966.

Frammenti di etica. Bari: Laterza, 1922. Reprinted in *Etica e politica,* 5–213. This book was translated by Arthur Livingston under the title *The Conduct of Life.* New York: Books for Libraries Press, 1967.

"Giambattista Vico primo scopritore della scienza estetica." Flegrea, 3d year, 2 (1901): 1–26, 97–116. Translated in *Aesthetic* (1958), 220–234.

Goethe con una scelta delle liriche nuovamente tradotte. 5th ed. 2 parts. Bari: Laterza, 1959. Part 1 was translated into English by E. Anderson with an introduction by D. Ainslie under the title *Goethe*. New York: Kennikat Press, 1970.

"L'immaterialismo del Berkeley." La critica: Rivista di letteratura, storia e filosofia 7 (1909): 77–81. Reprinted in *Conversazioni critiche*. 2d series, 109–15.

Indagini su Hegel e schiarimenti filosofici. 2d ed. Bari: Laterza, 1967.

"L'intuizione pura e il carattere lirico dell'arte." La critica: Rivista di letteratura, storia e filosofia 6 (1908): 248–50. Reprinted in *Problemi di estetica*, 3–30. This article was translated by D. Ainslie in the first edition (1909) of the *Aesthetic* but did not appear in the revised edition (1922).

"Intuizione, sentimento, liricità." La critica: Rivista di letteratura, storia e filosofia 5 (1907): 248–50. Reprinted in *Pagine sparse* 1 : 211–17.

Letture di poeti. 3d economic reprint of 1st ed. Bari: Laterza, 1966.

"Lineamenti di una logica come scienza del concetto puro." Atti dell' accademia pontaniana 35 (1905): 1–140. Croce considered this essay as the first edition of the *Logica*. Reprinted in *La prima forma della Estetica*, 119–312.

Logica come scienza del concetto puro. 9th ed. Bari: Laterza, 1963. The 2d edition (1909) was translated into English by D. Ainslie under the title *Logic as the Science of the Pure Concept*. London: Macmillan, 1917.

Materialismo storico ed economia marxistica. 10th ed. Bari: Laterza, 1961. Translated by C. M. Meredith, with an introduction by A. D. Lindsay, under the title *Historical Materialism and the Economics of Karl Marx*. New York: Russell & Russell, 1966.

Memorie della mia vita. Verona: Valdonega, 1966.

My Philosophy and Other Essays on the Moral and Political Problems of Our Time. Selected by R. Klibansky and translated by E. F. Carritt. London: George Allen & Unwin, 1951.

Nuove pagine sparse. 1st series, *Vita, pensiero, letteratura*. 2d series, *Metodologia, storiografica, osservazioni su libri nuovi—varietà*. Napoli: Riccardo Ricciardi, 1949.

Nuovi saggi di estetica. 4th ed. Bari: Laterza, 1958.

Pagine sparse. 2d ed. Vol. 1, *Letteratura e cultura*. Vol. 2, *Biografie; storia napoletana; schermaglie per varia occasione; ricordi di vita ministeriale; questioni del giorno; documenti storici*. Vol. 3, *Postille; osservazioni su libri nuovi*. Bari: Laterza, 1960.

La poesia: Introduzione alla critica e storia della poesia. 6th ed. Bari: Laterza, 1963. Translated by Giovanni Gullace under the title *Benedetto Croce's Poetry and Literature: An Introduction to Its Criticism and History*. Carbondale: Southern Illinois University Press, 1981.

Poesia antica e moderna: Interpretazioni. 5th ed. Bari: Laterza, 1966.

La poesia di Dante. 11th ed. Bari: Laterza, 1966. Translated by D. Ainslie under the title *The Poetry of Dante.* New York: Paul P. Appel, 1971.

Poesia e non poesia: Note sulla letteratura europea del secolo decimonono. 7th ed. Bari: Laterza, 1964. Translated by D. Ainslie under the title *European Literature in the Nineteenth Century.* London: Chapman & Hall, 1925.

Poesia popolare e poesia d'arte: Studi sulla poesia italiana dal tre al cinquecento. 5th ed. Bari: Laterza, 1967.

"Postilla alla lettera di R. Eisler." La critica: Rivista di letteratura, storia e filosofia 3 (1905): 86–88. Reprinted in *Pagine sparse* 1 : 204–9.

La prima forma della "Estetica" e della "Logica." Messina-Roma: Principato, 1924.

Primi saggi. 3d ed. Bari: Laterza, 1951.

Problemi di estetica e contributi alla storia dell'estetica italiana. 5th ed. Bari: Laterza, 1954.

"Il programma della Critica." La critica: Rivista di letteratura, storia e filosofia 1 (1903): 1–5. Reprinted in *Conversazioni critiche,* 2d series, 353–57.

Saggio sullo Hegel: Seguito da altri scritti di storia della filosofia. 5th ed. Bari: Laterza, 1967. This book includes *Ciò che è vivo e ciò che è morto della filosofia di Hegel* without its bibliography.

"Siamo noi hegeliani?" La critica: Rivista di letteratura, storia e filosofia 2 (1904): 261–64. Reprinted in *Cultura e vita morale,* 47–52.

La storia come pensiero e come azione. 7th ed. Bari: Laterza, 1965. The 3d edition without "final considerations," or the appendix and philological notes was translated by S. Sprigge under the title *History as the Story of Liberty.* New York: Noonday Press, 1955. Subsequently the section entitled *"La storia come pensiero e come azione,"* in *La storia,* 1–50, was retranslated by C. Sprigge in *Philosophy, Poetry, History,* 546–88.

Storia del Regno di Napoli. 6th ed. Bari: Laterza, 1965. Translated by F. Frenaye and edited with an introduction by H. Stuart Hughes under the title *History of the Kingdom of Naples.* Chicago: University of Chicago Press, 1970.

"Storia e autobiografia." La critica: Rivista di letteratura, storia e filosofia 26 (1928), 231–32.

Teoria e storia della storiografia. 9th ed. Bari: Laterza, 1966. The 2d edition (1919) was translated by D. Ainslie. It was published in England under the title *Theory and History of Historiography.* London: Harrap & Co., 1921. In America, its title was *History: Its Theory and Practice.* New York: Russell & Russell, 1921 (1960).

Terze pagine sparse. 2 vols. Bari: Laterza, 1955.

"Tesi fondamentali di un'Estetica come scienza dell'espressione e linguistica generale." Atti dell'accademia pontaniana 30 (1900): 1–88. Reprinted in *La prima forma della "Estetica,"* 1–118.

Ultimi saggi. 3d ed. Bari: Laterza, 1963.

2. CORRESPONDENCE

Lettere a Giovanni Gentile. Edited by Alda Croce with an introduction by Gennaro Sasso. Milano: Arnoldo Mondadori, 1981.

Critical Treatments of Croce's Thought

1. BOOKS

Abbate, M. *La filosofia di B. Croce e la crisi della società italiana.* Torino: Einaudi, 1966.

Agazzi, Emilio. *Il giovane Croce e il marxismo.* Torino: Einaudi, 1962.

Albeggiani, F. *Inizio e svolgimento della filosofia dello spirito di Benedetto Croce.* Palermo: Gino, 1960.

Aliotta, A. *La conoscenza intuitiva nell'estetica del Croce.* Piacenza: Bertola, 1904.

———. *L'estetica del Croce e la crisi dell'idealismo moderno.* Napoli: Perrella, 1917.

Antoni, Carlo. *Commento a Croce.* Venezia: Pozzi, 1955.

———. *Il tempo e le idee.* Napoli: Edizioni scientifiche italiane, 1968.

———. *Teoria e storia dello storiografia.* Vol. 1. Napoli: Edizioni scientifiche italiane, 1950.

Antonini, Fausto. *Il problema della storia del pensiero di Benedetto Croce.* Buzini, 1967.

Bartolomei, T. *Idealismo e realismo.* Torino: Marietti, 1938.

Barzini, L. *From Caesar to the Mafia.* London: Hamish Hamilton, 1971.

Battaglia, F. *Il problema della storia.* Milano: Bocca, 1944.

Bausola, A. *Etica e politica nel pensiero di Benedetto Croce.* Milano: Società editrice vita e pensiero, 1966.

———. *Filosofia e storia nel pensiero crociano.* Milano: Società editrice vita e pensiero, 1965.

Biscione, M. *Interpreti di Croce.* Napoli: Giannini, 1968.

Borgese, G. A. *La poetica dell'unità.* Milano: Treves, 1934.

Bosanquet, B. *Three Lectures on Aesthetic.* London: Macmillan & Co., 1915.

Brown, M. E. *Neo-Idealistic Aesthetics: Croce-Gentile-Collingwood.* Detroit: Wayne State University Press, 1966.

Bruno, Antonino. *La crisi dell'idealismo nell'ultimo Croce.* Bari: Laterza, 1964.

————. *Economia ed etica nello svolgimento del pensiero crociano.* Siracusa-Catania: Ciranna, 1958.

————. *Metologia e metafisica nel pensiero crociano.* Bologna: Leonardi, 1964.

Calogero, G. *La conclusione della filosofia del conoscere.* Firenze: Le Monnier, 1938.

————. *Estetica, semantica, istorica.* Torino: Einaudi, 1943.

————. *Studi crociani.* Rieti: Biblioteca, 1930.

Caponigri, A. Robert. *History and Liberty: The Historical Writings of Benedetto Croce.* London: Routledge and Kegan Paul, 1955.

Carbonara, C. *Sviluppo e problemi dell'estetica crociana.* Napoli: Humus, 1947.

Carnevale, L. *Il concetto puro della filosifia dello spirito e la storia del sec. XIX di B. Croce.* Varese: Arcivescovile, 1934.

Carr, H. W. *The Philosophy of Benedetto Croce.* New York: Russell & Russell, 1969.

Carritt, E. F. *The Theory of Beauty.* London: Methuen, 1914.

Caruso, E. F. *Per la critica dell'estetica e dell'idealismo crociano.* Siracusa: Arti grafiche santoro, 1949.

Castellano Giovanni. *Benedetto Croce.* Bari: Laterza, 1936.

————. *Introduzione allo studio delle opere di Benedetto Croce.* Bari: Laterza, 1920.

Ceccarini, E. *Benedetto Croce: La storia, la libertà.* Roma: Edizioni della voce, 1967.

Ciardo, M. *Marx e Croce.* Napoli: Generoso Procaccini, 1983.

————. *Le quattro epoche dello storicismo: Vico, Kant, Hegel, Croce.* Napoli: Generoso Procaccini, 1983.

Cione, E. *Benedetto Croce e il pensiero contemporaneo.* Milano: Longanesi, 1963.

————. *Benedetto Croce e la nuova filosofia.* Milano: Longanesi, 1962.

————. *Bibliografia crociana.* Roma: Fratelli Bocca, 1956.

Cohen, M. *The Meaning of Human History.* La Salle, Ill.: Open Court, 1947.

Collingwood, R. G. *The Idea of History.* London: Oxford University Press, 1946.

Colorni, E. *L'estetica di B. Croce.* Milano: La cultura, 1932.

Contini, Gianfranco. *L'influenza culturale di Benedetto Croce.* Milano and Napoli: Ricciardi, 1967.

Corsi, M. *Le origini del pensiero di Benedetto Croce.* Firenze: La nuova italia, 1951.

Crespi, Angelo. *Contemporary Thought of Italy.* New York: Knopf, 1926.

Croce, Elena. *L'infanzia dorata e recordi familiari.* Milano: Adelphi, 1979.

Cuccaro, J. *L'opera filosofica, storica e letteraria di B. Croce.* Bari: Laterza, 1941.

De Feo, Italo. *Benedetto Croce e il suo mondo.* Torino: Edizioni rai radiotelevisione italiana, 1966.

De Gennaro, Angelo A. *The Philosophy of Benedetto Croce.* New York: Citadel Press, 1961.

De Gennaro, Giovanni. *Il concetto della unità delle arti nella estetica di Benedetto Croce.* Molfetti: Messina, 1969.

De Ruggiero, Guido. *Modern Philosophy,* trans. A. H. Hannay and R. G. Collingwood. New York: Macmillan, 1921.

Faucci, D. *Storicismo e metafisica nel pensiero crociano.* Firenze: La nuova italia, 1950.

Flora, F., ed. *Benedetto Croce.* Milano: Malfasi, 1953.

Franchini, R. *Croce interprete di Hegel: e altri saggi filosofici.* Napoli: Giannini, 1964.

———. *Esperienza dello storicismo.* Napoli: Giannini, 1964.

———. *Intervista su Croce.* Napoli: Società editrice napoletana, 1978.

———. *Metafisica e storia.* Napoli: Giannini, 1958.

———. *L'oggetto della filosofia.* Napoli: Giannini, 1967.

———. *Le origini della dialettica.* Napoli: Giannini, 1965.

———. *La teoria della storia di Benedetto Croce.* Napoli: Morano, 1966.

Galasso, Giuseppe. *Croce, Gramsci, e altri storici.* Milano: Mondadori, 1969.

Gancitano, Cosimo. *Critica dell'estetica crociana.* Mazara: Società editrice siciliana, 1948.

Garibaldi, Rinaldo. *Genesis e svolgimento storico delle primi tesi estetiche di B. Croce.* Firenze: Fussi, 1949.

Gentile, G. *Filosofia dell'arte.* Milano: Treves, 1931.

———. *La filosofia italiana contemporanea.* Firenze: Sansoni, 1941.

———. *Frammenti di estetica e letteratura.* Lanciano: Carabba, 1920.

Gramsci, A. *Il materialismo storico e la filosofia di Benedetto Croce.* Torino: Einaudi, 1949.

Harris, H. S. *The Social Philosophy of Giovanni Gentile.* Urbana: University of Illinois Press, 1960.

Jacobitti, Edmund E. *Revolutionary Humanism and Historicism in Modern Italy.* New Haven: Yale University Press, 1981.

Jannazzo, Antonio. *Croce e il comunismo.* Napoli: Edizioni scientifiche italiane, 1982.

Lamanna, E. *Introduzione alla lettura di Croce.* Firenze: Felice le monnier, 1969.

Lanza, Adriano. *Benedetto Croce: Breviario d'estetica.* Roma: Le muse, 1969.

Lentini, Giacinto. *Croce e Gramsci.* Palermo and Roma: Mori, 1967.

Levi, G. *Studi estetici.* Lapi: Città di castello, 1967.

Lombardi, A. *La filosofia di Benedetto Croce.* Roma: Bardi, 1946.

Mandelbaum, M. *The Anatomy of Historical Knowledge.* Baltimore: Johns Hopkins University Press, 1977.

————. *Philosophy, History, and the Sciences.* Baltimore: Johns Hopkins University Press, 1984.

————. *The Problem of Historical Knowledge.* New York: Liveright, 1938.

Manna, Ambrogio. *Lo storicismo di Benedetto Croce.* Napoli: D'Auria, 1965.

Mossini, L. *La categoria dell'unità nel pensiero di Benedetto Croce.* Milano: Giuffre, 1959.

Murray, G.; Brosio, M.; and Calogero, G. *Studi crociani.* London: Westerham Press, 1953.

Nicolini, F. *Benedetto Croce.* Torino: Unione tipografico–editrice torinese, 1962.

————. *Benedetto Croce: Vita intellettuale.* Napoli: Cacciavillani, 1944.

Orsini, Gian N. G. *Benedetto Croce: Philosopher of Art and Literary Critic.* Carbondale: Southern Illinois University Press, 1961.

Palmer, L. M., and Harris, H. S., eds. *Thought, Action and Intuition: A Symposium on the Philosophy of Benedetto Croce.* Hildesheim and New York: George Olms, 1975.

Paolozzi, Ernesto. *I problemi dell'estetica italiana.* Napoli: Società editrice napoletana, 1985.

Pardo, F. *La filosofia teoretica di B. Croce.* Napoli: Perrella, 1928.

Parente, A. *Croce per lumi sparsi. Problemi e ricordi.* Firenze: La nuova italia, 1975.

————. *La musica e le arti.* Bari: Laterza, 1936.

————. *L'opera filosofica, storica e letteraria di B. Croce.* Bari: Laterza, 1941.

Pesce, Domenico. *L'estetica dopo Croce.* Firenze: Philosophia, 1962.

Petruzzellis, N. *Il problema della storia nell'idealismo moderno.* 2d ed. Firenze: Sansoni, 1940.

————. *Sistema e problema.* Bari: Laterza, 1954.

Piazza, Giuseppe. *L'errore come atto logico.* Bari: Laterza, 1924.

Piccoli, Raffaello. *Benedetto Croce: An Introduction to His Philosophy*. New York: Harcourt, Brace & Co., 1922.

Puppo, M. *Benedetto Croce e la critica letteraria*. Firenze: Sansoni, 1974.

———. *Il metodo e la critica di Benedetto Croce*. Milano: Murcia, 1964.

Roggerone, Giuseppe A. *Benedetto Croce e la fondazione del concetto di libertà*. Milano: Marzorati, 1966.

———. *Prospettive crociane*. Lecce: Milella, 1968.

Romanell, P. (See Romanelli, P.) *Croce versus Gentile*. New York: S. F. Vanni, 1938.

Romanelli, P. *The Philosophy of Giovanni Gentile*. New York: S. F. Vanni, 1938.

Romano, P. *Influssi del pensiero kantiano nell'estetica di B. Croce*. Bari: Accolti, 1938.

Romano, Salvatore F. *Il concetto di storia nella filosofia di Benedetto Croce*. Palermo: Editore Trimarchi, 1933.

Rossani, W. *Croce e l'estetica*. Milano: Pan, 1971.

Russo, L. *La critica letteraria contemporanea*. Bari: Laterza, 1942.

Sansone, Mario. *Interpretazioni crociane*. Bari: Laterza, 1965.

Saragat, G. *On the Centenary of the Birth of Benedetto Croce*. New York: Istituto italiano di cultura, 1966.

Sasso, G. *Benedetto Croce: La ricerca della dialettica*. Napoli: Morano, 1975.

———. *Passato e presente nella storia della filosofia*. Bari: Laterza, 1967.

Seervelt, C. G. *Benedetto Croce's Earlier Aesthetic Theories and Literary Criticism: A Critical Philosophical Look at the Development during his Rationalistic Years*. Kampen, Netherlands: J. H. Kok, 1958.

Sgroi, C. *Gli studi estetici in Italia*. Firenze: La nuova italia, 1932.

———. *Svolgimento storico della sua estetica*. Messina: D'Anna, 1947.

Spingarn, J. *Creative Criticism: Essays on the Unity of Genius and Taste*. New York: Henry Holt and Co., 1917.

———. *Creative Criticism and Other Essays*. New York: Harcourt Brace, 1931.

Spirito, U. *L'idealismo italiano e i suoi critici*. Firenze: Le monnier, 1930.

———. *Il nuovo idealismo italiano*. Roma: Alberti, 1923.

Sprigge, C. *Benedetto Croce: Man and Thinker*. Cambridge: Bowes & Bowes, 1952.

Tanga, Iginio. *L'estetica di Benedetto Croce*. Roma: Copa, 1959.

Ungari, G. P. *Croce in Francia*. Napoli: Istituto italiano, 1967.

Valentini, F. *La contrariforma della dialettica*. Roma: Riuniti, 1966.

Vitiello, V. *Storiografia e storia nel pensiero di Benedetto Croce*. Napoli: Libreria scientifica editrice, 1968.

Walkley, A. *Dramatic Criticism*. London: John Murray, 1903.

Wellek, René. *Four Critics: Croce, Valéry, Lukács, and Ingarden*. Seattle: University of Washington Press, 1981.

Zacchi, A. *Il nuovo idealismo di B. Croce e G. Gentile*. Roma: Ferrari, 1925.

2. ARTICLES

Agosti, Vittorio. *"Due commentari allo storicismo del Croce." Giornale di metafisica* 24 (1969): 469–75.

Allen, George. "Croce's Theory of Historical Judgment: A Reassessment." *The Modern Schoolman* 1–2 (Jan. 1975): 169–87.

Arisato, Hiroshi. *"Pensiero del De Sanctis e del Croce sull' Ariosto." Studi italici* (Kyoto) 15 (Dec. 1966): 45–56.

Assunto, Rosario. *"La revisione critica del pensiero crociano e il problema della categoria estetica."* In *Interpretazioni crociane*, 5–106. Bari: Adriatica editrice, 1965.

Attisani, Adelchi. *"Introduzione all'Estetica di Benedetto Croce." Letterature moderne* 2 (1961): 440–60.

———. *"Gli studi di estetica."* In *Cinquant' anni di vita intellettuale italiana, 1896–1946,* 290ff. Napoli: Edizioni scientifiche italiane, 1950.

———. *"Svolgimento del pensiero estetico di B. Croce, III." Letterature moderne* 2 (1961): 569–85.

Battaglia, Felice. *"Rassegna di studi crociani." Giornale di metafisica* 19 (1964): 718–36.

Bausola, Adriano. *"Immanenza e individualità in Benedetto Croce." Studium* 62 (1966): 494–505.

Bertocci, A. P. "The Development of Croce's Aesthetic." *Boston University Graduate Journal* 10 (1962): 86–95, 127–39.

Biondolillo, Francesco. *"Benedetto Croce: Nel centenario della sua nascita." Ausonia* 21 (1) (1966): 47–52.

Blocker, H. Gene. "Another Look at Aesthetic Imagination." *Journal of Aesthetics and Art Criticism* 30 (1972): 529–36.

Bosanquet, B. "Douglas Ainslie's Logic as a Science of Pure Concept." *Mind* 27 : 475–84.

Brescia, Giuseppe. *"I primi scritti di Benedetto Croce." Cultura* 9 (1971): 279–81.

Brown, Merle E. "Croce's Early Aesthetics: 1894–1912." *Journal of Aesthetics and Art Criticism* 22 (1963): 29–41.

Bruno, Antonino. *"L'esistenzialismo e la forma economica in Croce." Historica* (1951): 3–15.

————. *"La formazione crociana dei distinti e le ultime indagini sulla vitalità e la dialettica."* In *Benedetto Croce,* ed. Francesco Flora. Milano: Malfasi, 1953.

————. *"Metodologia e metafisica nel pensiero italiano contemporaneo."* Rivista interna di filosofia politica e sociale (1964): 299–312.

————. *"Una lettera sul problema della vitalità."* La rivista di studi crociani 7 (1971): 283–86.

Calogero, G. *"Postilla ai ricordi crociani."* Cultura 5 (1967): 166–79.

————. *"Ricordi e riflessioni: Benedetto Croce."* Cultura 4 (1966): 145–79.

Caponigri, A. Robert. "Croce, Benedetto." In *Encyclopaedia Britannica.* 15th ed., 1974.

Carus, P. "Croce's Use of the Word 'Intuition.'" *The Monist* 26 (1916): 312–15.

Ciardo, Manlio. *"Marx e Croce ieri e oggi."* La rivista di studi crociani 17 (1980): 362–70; 18 (1981): 32–50.

Colucci, Federico. *"I fondamenti della crociana teoria dell'errore e i problemi del marxismo negli anni 1895–1900."* La rivista di studi crociani 15 (1978): 275–85.

Corsano, Antonia. *"Croce e la storia della filosofia."* In *Interpretazioni crociane,* 153–169. Bari: Adriatica editrice, 1965.

Cotroneo, Girolamo. *"La teoria della distinzione e i suoi nemici."* La rivista di studi crociani 18 (1981): 146–67.

Croce, Elena. *"Ricordi familiari su Benedetto Croce."* Letterature moderne 12 (1962): 349–58.

De Gennaro, Angelo A. "An Approach to Benedetto Croce." *The Personalist* 42 (1961): 21–27.

————. "Croce and Collingwood." *The Personalist* 46 (1965): 193–202.

————. "Croce and De Sanctis." *Journal of Aesthetics and Art Criticism* 23 (1964–65): 228–31.

————. "Croce and Hegel." *The Personalist* 44 (1963): 302–6.

————. "Croce and Marx." *The Personalist* 43 (1962): 466–72.

————. "Croce and Vico." *Journal of Aesthetics and Art Criticism* 22 (1963): 43–46.

————. "Vico and Croce: The Genesis of Croce's Aesthetics." *The Personalist* 50 (1969): 508–25.

De Grandi, Marcello. *"Coordinate estetico–critiche crociane."* Letture 21 (1966): 651–84.

————. *"Incidenza della filosofia di Croce nella sua opera critica I–II."* Filosofia e vita 4 (1963): 59–78; 5 (1964): 61–67.

————. *"La totalità dell'espressione artistica e della riforma della storia letteraria in Benedetto Croce (1917–1936)" Filosofia e vita* 5 (1964): 28–42, 79–87.

De Mauro, Tullio. *"La letteratura critica più recente sull'estetica e la linguistica crociana." De homine* 11–12 (1964): 273–86.

Destler, Chester McArthur. "The Crocean Origin of Becker's Historical Relativism." *History and Theory: Studies in the Philosophy of History* 9 (1970): 335–42.

Dimler, G. R., S. J. "Creative Intuition in the Aesthetic Theories of Croce and Maritain." *The New Scholasticism* 37 (1963): 472–92.

Donagan, A. H. "Collingwood's Debt to Croce." *Mind* 81 (1972): 265–66.

Dondoli, Luciano. *"Note sul pensiero storiografico di Benedetto Croce." Scuola e cultura nel mondo* 43 (1966): 5–27.

Douglas, George H. "Croce's Early Aesthetic and American Critical Theory." *Comparative Literature Studies* 7 (1970): 204–15.

————. "Croce's Expression Theory of Art Revisited." *The Personalist* 54 (1973): 60–70.

————. "A Reconsideration of the Dewey-Croce Exchange." *Journal of Aesthetics and Art Criticism* 28 (1970): 497–504.

Fagone, Virgilio. *"Ciò che è vivo e ciò che è morto della filosofia di Benedetto Croce." Civiltà cattolica* 117 (1966): 421–33.

Fantini, Stefano. *"Carlo Antoni e lo storicismo crociano." La rivista di studi crociani* 20 (1983): 140–51.

Fisch, Max H. *"Croce e Vico." La rivista di studi crociani* 5 (1968): 9–30, 151–71.

Flora, Francesco. *"Occasioni e aperture: De Sanctis, Croce e la critica contemporanea." Letterature moderne* 2 (1961): 5–33.

Franchini, R. *"Croce e la metodologia storiografia." In Interpretazioni crociane* 169–95. Bari: Adriatica editrice, 1965.

————. *"La dialettica 'negativa.'" La rivista di studi crociani* 8 (1971): 253–59.

Gullace, Giovanni. "Poetry and Literature in Croce's *La poesia." Journal of Aesthetics and Art Criticism* 19 (1961): 453–61.

Guzzo, Augusto. *"Itinerario estetico." Filosofia* 23 (1972): 349–74.

Hack, R. "The Doctrine of Literary Forms." *Harvard Studies in Classical Philology,* ed. The Committee of the Classical Instructors of Harvard University, 27 (1916): 1–65.

Harris, H. S. "Croce, Benedetto." In *Encyclopedia of Philosophy,* ed. Paul Edwards, 2:263–67. New York: Macmillan, 1972.

—————. "What Is Living and What Is Dead in the Philosophy of Croce?" *Dialogue* 6 (1967): 399–405.

Mandelbaum, Maurice. "The History of Philosophy: Some Methodological Issues." *Journal of Philosophy* 74 (10) (1977): 561–72.

Mantovani, Giuseppe. *"Croce: Filosofia e il marxismo." Vita e pensiero* 49 (1966): 838–54.

Milburn, M. M. "Benedetto Croce's Coherence Theory of Truth: A Critical Evaluation." *Filosofia* 19 (1968): 107–76 (in bound volumes, 725–34).

Montale, Eugenio, *"L'estetica e la critica." Mondo* 14 (1) (1962): 3–4.

—————. "Lesson on Croce: Esthetics and Criticism." *Italian Quarterly* 7 (1963): 48–65.

Moss, M. E. "Croce's Theory of Intuition Reconsidered." *La rivista di studi crociani* 15 (1978): 292–306.

—————. "The Enduring Values in the Philosophy of Benedetto Croce." *Idealistic Studies* 10 (1980): 46–66.

—————. "Petrarch and Modern Criticism: De Sanctis and Croce." *Rivista rosminiana di filosofia e di cultura* (Jan.–Mar. 1977): 35–42.

Oberti, Elisa. *"Valore storico e teoretico delle proposte estetiche di Croce." Vita e pensiero* 49 (1966): 507–14.

Orsini, Gian N. G. *"Coleridge e Croce: Note di estetica e di critica della poesia." La rivista di studi crociani* 4 (1964): 444–53.

—————. "Recent Accounts of Croce." *Italian Quarterly* 5 (1961): 61–64.

Paci, E. *"Benedetto Croce: Intorno al Hegel e alla dialettica." Archivio di filosofia (filosofia e psicopatologia),* no. 6 (1952): 560.

Parente, A. *"Il concetto crociano della vitalità." La rivista di studi crociani* 7 (1970): 399–409.

—————. *"Estetica e gusto nell'opera critica di Croce." La rivista di studi crociani* 3 (1966): 283–94.

—————. *"Intorno al concetto crociano di 'vitale': Storia e sostanza di un'interpretazione." La rivista di studi crociani* 8 (1971): 1–13.

—————. *"Lineamenti del concetto di dialettica." La rivista di studi crociani* 7 (1970): 263–86.

—————. *"Malinconia di Croce—un raro inedito del filosofo." La rivista di studi crociani* 19 (1982): 325–7.

—————. *"Le ragioni dinamiche del circolo spirituale e il così detto 'passagio' tra le forme." La rivista di studi crociani* 18 (1981): 249–54.

—————. *"Risposta al Bruno sullo stesso tema." La rivista di studi crociani* 8 (1971): 287–97.

————. *"Sul concetto di 'contemporaneità' della storia."* La rivista di studi crociani 18 (1981): 361–67.

Patanker, R. B. "What Does Croce Mean by 'Expression'?" *British Journal of Aesthetics* 2 (1962): 112–25.

Perricone Jr., Christopher. "The Place of Idiom in Benedetto Croce's Theory of Aesthetic." *La rivista di studi crociani* 20 (1983): 41–62.

Petruzzellis, N. *"B. Croce, indagini su Hegel e schiarimenti filosofici."* Rassegna di scienze filosofiche, no. 2 (1952): 155.

Puppo, Mario. *"La metodologia del Croce e le tendenze della recente critica letteraria."* Studium 62 (1966): 520–27.

Read, Sir Herbert. "The Essence of Beauty." *John O'London's Weekly* (July 6, 1961): 3.

Reynolds, Barbara. "Benedetto Croce." *Times* (London), Oct. 3, 1963: 15.

Rizzacasa, Aurelio. *"Significato e valore dell'indagine storica (riflessioni critiche sul pensiero di B. Croce)."* Sapienza 17 (1964): 244–52.

Rossani, Volfango. *"La critica figurativa e l'estetica crociana."* Osservatore politico letterario 7 (2) (1961): 84–102.

Russo, Luigi, and Parente, Alfredo. *"La polemica fra Croce e Dewey e l'arte come esperienza."* La rivista di studi crociani 5 (1968): 201–27.

Samana, P. *"B. Croce, il concetto della storia."* Quaderni di cultura e studi sociali, no. 6–7 (1954): 468.

Santoli, V. *"Benedetto Croce, filosofia poesia storia."* Rivista di letterature moderne, no. 1 (1952): 60.

Sasso, Gennaro. *"Due variazioni polemiche sull'interpretazione di Croce."* Cultura 6 (1968): 260–76.

————. *"Filosofia e storiografia in Benedetto Croce."* Cultura 2 (1964): 30–54.

Semerari, Giuseppe. *"Croce e la filosofia."* Giornale critico della filosofia italiana 45 (1966): 467–84.

————. *"Storia e storiografia in Croce."* Aut aut 83 (1965): 42–52.

Sprigge, Cecil. "Benedetto Croce: Man and Thinker." In B. Croce, *Philosophy, Poetry, History,* trans. C. Sprigge, ix–lxxi. London: Oxford University Press, 1966.

Steinman, James L. "Santayana and Croce: An Aesthetic Reconciliation." *Journal of Aesthetics and Art Criticism* 30 (1971): 251–53.

Stella, Vittorio. *"Il giudizio e la prassi: Studi su Croce dal 1971 al 1975."* Cultura 14 (1976): 312–51.

————. *"Il giudizio su Croce: Consuntivo di un centenario."* Giornale di metafisica 22 (1967): 643–711.

————. *"Interpretazioni sull'utile e il vitale nel pensiero crociano."* Giornale di metafisica 17 (1962): 29–71.

Terenzio, Vincenzo. *"Fenomenologia dell'errore."* La rivista di studi crociani 19 (1982): 366–72.

Tertulian, Nicolas. *"Introduzione all'estetica di Croce."* La rivista di studi crociani 8 (1971): 138–53, 378–94.

Tessitore, Fulvio. *"Storicismo hegeliano e storicismo crociano."* In Incidenza di Hegel, ed. F. Tessitore, 845–910. Napoli: Morsano, 1970.

Tholfsen, Trygve R. "What Is Living in Croce's Theory of History?" *Historian* 23 (1961): 288–302.

White, Hayden V. "The Abiding Relevance of Croce's Idea of History." *Journal of Modern History* 35 (1963): 109–24.

————. "Croce and Becker: A Note on the Evidence of Influence." *History and Theory: Studies in the Philosophy of History* 10 (1971): 222–27.

————. "What Is Living and What Is Dead in Croce's Criticism of Vico." In *Giambattista Vico: An International Symposium*, ed. Giorgio Tagliacozzo and Hayden V. White, 379–90. Baltimore: Johns Hopkins University Press, 1969.

Index